FLYING UP THE EDGWARE ROAD

THE BIRTH OF NORTH-WEST LONDON'S AVIATION INDUSTRY

MARK AMIES

AMBERLEY

Dedicated to my late father, Nick Amies

Cover images: 1919 Airco press ad illustration (Aviation Ancestry), 1919 Airco publicity postcard. (Barnet Local Studies)

Rear cover image 1: A 1920s advertisement for the London Aeroplane Club, Stag Lane. (Author's collection)

Rear cover image 2: Women aircraft workers at the Grahame-White factory applying dope to aircraft wings. (Barnet Local Studies)

First published 2022

Amberley Publishing
The Hill, Stroud,
Gloucestershire, GL5 4EP

www.amberley-books.com

Copyright © Mark Amies, 2022

ISBN: 978 1 3981 0946 9 (print)
ISBN: 978 1 3981 0947 6 (ebook)

British Library Cataloguing in Publication Data.
A catalogue record for this book is available from the British Library.

Typeset in 10pt on 13pt Celeste.
Typesetting by SJmagic DESIGN SERVICES, India.
Printed in the UK.

Contents

Introduction

In my first book, *London's Industrial Past*, I looked at a broad selection of industries that existed around the capital city over the course of the twentieth century. This time I have decided to focus on one industry, in one area. Although London had a large number of aircraft makers dotted across its expanse, a section of the Edgware Road had a particularly heavy concentration. My objective is to illustrate how aviation arrived into the north-west fringes of London and changed it forever, from the early days of the pioneer aeronauts, flying from

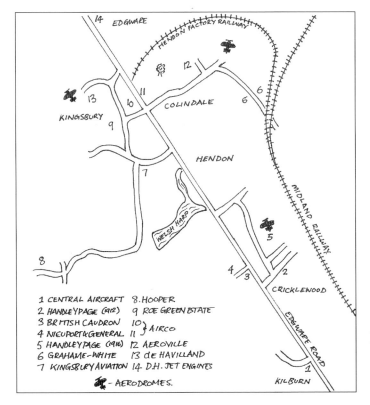

A basic map showing the locations of the main aircraft constructors and aerodromes (not to scale).

rough pasture land, through the rapid industrialisation of the First World War, and on into the years after, when the legacy of the aircraft industry made its mark on north-west London. We go from Kilburn to Edgware, and our main focus of activity is the early years of the twentieth century. Out of the seven aircraft makers we look at, only two managed to survive into the 1960s – the other five had closed by the 1920s. The factory spaces they left behind were inherited by other types of manufacturing, and more importantly, the highly skilled and efficient workforce were able to take their skill sets into new areas in the peacetime years of the 1920s and '30s.

Along the Edgware Road in 1901

The Edgware Road is an ancient route that runs from Marble Arch, in the west end of Central London, out to Edgware in the north-west of Greater London. The route was part of a Roman road, also known as Watling Street, that started at Dover and ended in Holyhead, but it is likely that some of it predates the Romans, and it may have been a prehistoric trackway. It is interesting that a route so steeped in London's ancient history should find itself part of the development of something as radically new as aviation. Along its route from Kilburn, through to Cricklewood, on to Hendon, Colindale and eventually Edgware were based a number of early aircraft makers. However, in 1901, the start of the Edwardian era, the aeroplane had yet to make its impact on this part of Middlesex, which itself wasn't part of London until 1965.

The start of our journey is Kilburn High Road, the oldest part of our route and well established with shops and homes, and from here we head along Shoot Up Hill and arrive in Cricklewood Broadway. By 1901 Cricklewood was developing into a well-to-do Edwardian suburb, and as the century progressed the area would become home to many new industries. Leaving Cricklewood we pass the freight yards of the Midland Railway, which handled huge amounts of freight and coal. We descend, reaching the Brent Reservoir, better known as the Welsh Harp, which was created in the early 1800s by damming the River Brent, and acted as a water feeder for the Grand Union Canal. It took its name from the coaching hostelry on the side of Edgware Road, the Old Welsh Harp Inn. The road starts to rise again as we reach what was in 1901 the relatively new community of West Hendon. It was here that the mineral water bottling company of Schweppes built a new factory in 1896.

Moving along we arrive at the junction of Kingsbury Road. It is from this point that the Edgware Road becomes The Hyde, a name originating from a large house of the same name that stood nearby. As we carry on the road climbs quite noticeably, and in 1901 this section would have been open arable land; the road names running off it now allude to its past, as areas of hay-making – Sheaveshill and Hay Lane in particular. We then reach Colindale, its name associated with the Collin family who owned Collindale Lodge and land along Colindeep Lane. The double L was dropped at some point in the early twentieth century. The next road junction on The Hyde is Colindale Avenue, at the time a rather unassuming right of way that will eventually lead to the site of the London Aerodrome. It was on this road in 1901 that the company of Garstin Ltd built a leather trunk factory and workers' housing, called Leatherville. Nearby was the London Asylum. Built in 1898 in open Middlesex countryside, it would have been ideal for recuperation. Heading back onto The Hyde, past the turning for Colindale Avenue, was Hendon tram depot, opposite the estate of Grove Park, and Shoelands Farm, both of which will see great changes in the next two decades.

From this point the Edgware Road rises up again, dropping the section name of The Hyde, as it approaches what is now Burnt Oak. The road junction with Watling Avenue on one side and Stag Lane on the other would look very different in 1901. Watling Avenue was created in the early 1920s to take traffic and pedestrians to the new Underground station and the London County Council housing estate, built around the same time. Stag Lane, however, was a much older route, passing through farmland and on to Kingsbury. Returning to the Edgware Road, and from here to Edgware would have been through a large expanse of agricultural land and occasional houses. Before reaching the end of Edgware High Street, on the right-hand side of the road was the Hendon Union Workhouse, built in 1838, which later became Redhill Hospital and then Edgware Hospital. Edgware in 1901 was a linear settlement serving the carriage trade that plied the ancient roadway. Inns were dotted either side of the route, catering for travellers. Just as we reach the end of our journey we get to the area of Stonegrove, just outside Edgware, and in 1901 this would have been open fields and sports grounds. We have reached the end of our Edwardian journey, and in the next chapter we will see how the arrival of the pioneer aviators affected the area.

The Aviators Arrive

This book is as much about the pioneers of aviation as it is about the impact that the aviation industry made upon the landscape and economy of north-west London. It is the daring, bold and enterprising efforts that these individuals made that sealed the fate of Hendon as the epicentre of the changes that were to happen.

It is popularly assumed that the first successful flights started with the American brothers Wilbur and Orville Wright in December 1903. However, before powered winged flight, hot-air balloons carried people into the sky. Hendon's connection with flying originates with such craft, when in August 1862 Henry Tracey Coxwell and a party of four made a night-time landing in a field near Mill Hill. They had taken off from Crystal Palace in *The Mammoth*, heading to Biggleswade in Bedfordshire. Whilst Coxwell stayed with the balloon, the others walked on to the Greyhound Inn next to St Mary's Church to rest, returning early in the morning to resume their flight.

In the following years a number of hot-air balloon flights were made from the land around the Welsh Harp reservoir. The Welsh Harp had an association with recreational activities going back to 1858 when William Warner purchased the Old Welsh Harp Inn which was situated to the side of the Edgware Road, not far from the current Staples Corner junction. Warner invested heavily over the thirty years of his ownership, creating tea gardens and pleasure grounds, as well as a great many other activities. After Warner's ownership the Old Welsh Harp settled down to a more civilised period, and it was in the unused ballroom of the inn that Helmut Paul Martin and Cricklewood resident George Harris Handasyde began building an aeroplane in 1908. It is believed that the aircraft was hoisted up to the rafters, should the room be needed for its intended purpose. (Source: Martin Gegg, *Brooklands Bulletin*, Issue 66, Winter 2020.) The two men began trials of their aircraft in fields near the Welsh Harp, but these proved unsuccessful; in fact things went very badly at one point, when the engine dislodged itself from the machine whilst turning the large metal propellor. Martin and Handasyde gave up and continued their work at Brooklands aerodrome in Surrey. They set up a factory nearby in Woking and by the start of the First World War had renamed their company Martinsyde, going on to become a prominent volume manufacturer of military aircraft.

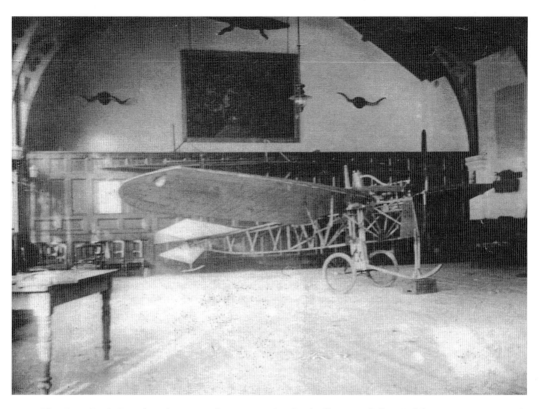

The Martin & Handasyde monoplane No. 1 in the ballroom of the Welsh Harp Inn, *c.* 1908. (Philip Jarrett Collection)

Almost at the same time that Martin and Handasyde were working on their aircraft at the Welsh Harp, another partnership was trying to produce their own flying machine, and it is their small contribution that was to be the very ignition point of Hendon's place in aviation history. E. J. Everett and Kenelm Edgcumbe were owners of Everett, Edgcumbe and Company, an electrical instrument manufacturer, with a factory in Colindeep Lane, just off the Edgware Road at Colindale. Mr Edgcumbe had taken an interest in aviation and decided to create his own aeroplane, and looking for a suitable area near their works to construct and fly an aircraft, discovered a piece of land at the end of Colindale Avenue. At that time it was open pasture used for dairy grazing and owned by three different individuals: Brinckman, Barham, and Brewer. During January 1910 trees were felled to clear more open space and the following month Hendon Urban District Council gave permission for a wooden shed to be built on the field, to house the aircraft. Edgcumbe contracted F. Smith & Co. of Stratford, East London, to build what became known as a hangar, and this rather inauspicious wooden structure would be the first building on what would later become the London Aerodrome.

The Everett and Edgcumbe monoplane was very much a locally produced effort, bringing in the talents of the West Hendon drapers Hawkers (no relation to the later famous aircraft manufacturer) to provide the wing fabric and stitching. The aircraft was powered by a four-cylinder 35 horsepower JAP petrol engine, made in Tottenham. Kenelm Edgcumbe was

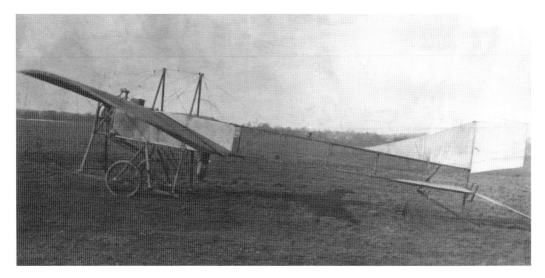

The Everett & Edgcumbe 'Grasshopper' at Hendon, *c.* 1910. (Philip Jarrett Collection)

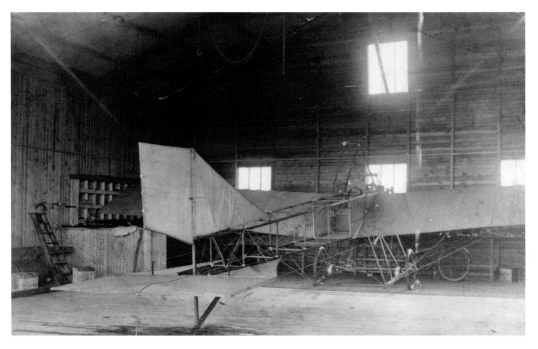

The Everett & Edgcumbe 'Grasshopper' in its wooden hangar, *c.* 1910. (Philip Jarrett Collection)

not short of assistance in his endeavour and one of his volunteers was Charles Richard Fairey, a twenty-two-year-old from Hendon. Fairey eventually formed his own aircraft company in 1915, which went on to produce the famous Swordfish torpedo aircraft of the Second World War, and the record-breaking Fairey Delta 2 jet. Flight testing of the Edgcumbe aircraft started in December 1910, carrying on through to the early part of 1911, but it never achieved more than a few tentative hops across the rough land. It was this behaviour that gave it the nickname 'The Grasshopper'. Local interest was high and crowds of spectators would converge on the fields to see the machine whenever word got out that it was being tested.

In April 1910 the *Daily Mail* held a London to Manchester air race, and one of the contestants, a Frenchman called Louis Paulhan, used the Everett and Edgcumbe hangar to house his Farman biplane and made the flying grounds at Hendon his base. His rival, a dashing young Englishman called Claude Grahame-White, flew from Park Royal in West London, but in the end it was Paulhan who would win. Grahame-White had begun his fascination with flight in balloons, and after attending Europe's first aviation meeting at Rheims in France in August 1909, he became obsessed with powered flight. By December 1909, after very little training, Claude Grahame-White acquired his French pilot's licence at Pau, and gained a British licence in April 1910.

On the Whit weekend holiday in May 1910 an impromptu air display took place at what had now become known as the 'Hendon Aviation Grounds'. Kenelm Edgcumbe was joined by a Mr A. Rawlinson, who arrived with his Farman biplane. Over the course of the weekend crowds had assembled to see the activities, which also included a large balloon from Crystal Palace floating past. As well as the aerial activity there were songs, dancing and music going on into the night. It would be a prequel to more organised events in future years.

By September 1910 Kenelm Edgcumbe and his brother-in-law purchased leases on the land and created the London Aerodrome Company Limited. More land was cleared and more sheds were built by F. Smith and Co., and it was not long before businesses would

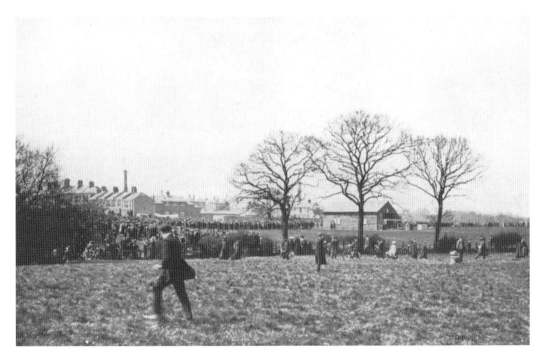

Crowds assembled to see Paulhan at Hendon, 1910. The Everett & Edgcumbe hangar is behind the middle tree. Within a year the trees would be felled and the fields levelled. The houses are on Colindale Avenue and in the distance is the Colindale Asylum. (Barnet Local Studies)

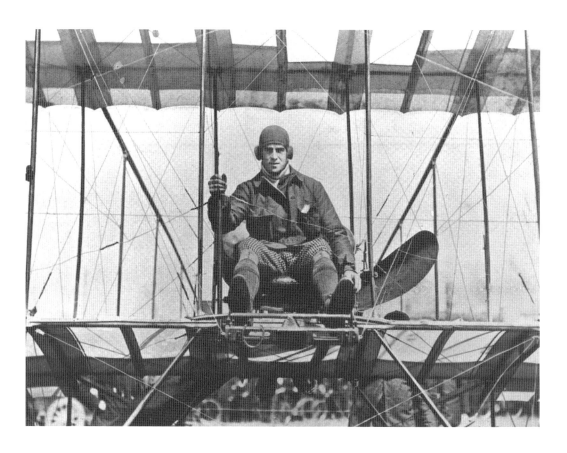

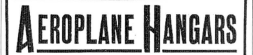

AEROPLANE HANGARS

Also Wood, Iron and Composite
Buildings of every description.
PLANS AND ESTIMATES FREE.

LOW PRICES. FIRST-CLASS WORK

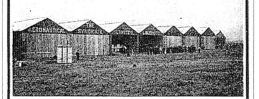

BUILDERS OF LONDON AERODROME
FOR THE LONDON AERODROME, LTD.
Surveyor waits on intending purchasers free of charge.

F. SMITH & CO.,

CARPENTER'S ROAD, STRATFORD, LONDON, E.

Telephone: STRATFORD 594. Telegrams: IRONIARUM, LONDON.

Above: Claude Grahame-White in his Farman biplane, *c.* 1910. (Barnet Local Studies)

Left: F. Smith & Co. advertisement featuring their hangars at Hendon, *c.* 1911. The Everett & Edgcumbe 'shed' is at the extreme right. (Aviation Ancestry)

inhabit them. The first notable enterprises were Horatio Barber's Aeronautical Syndicate and the Bleriot School of Flying, both prominently displaying their names on the front of the buildings in big white letters.

Claude Grahame-White returned to Hendon in January 1911, having moved his operations from Brooklands. He had ambitions to develop the flying grounds at Hendon into an internationally recognised aviation facility. He attempted to create a company with Louis Bleriot and Sir Henry Maxim, the early British aviation pioneer and developer of the machine gun. The subsequent share flotation failed, and Grahame-White decided to go it alone, forming the Grahame-White Aviation Company with financial assistance from his uncle and Sir Arthur Du Cros, who was the chairman of the Dunlop Tyre Company. By March 1911 the ownership of the London Aerodrome transferred to Claude Grahame-White, and a ten-year lease on the 207-acre site was acquired, with rights to purchase further land. Work was then undertaken by Grahame-White's business partner Richard Gates. Fields were cleared of trees and obstructions, watercourses diverted and culverted, and land drains installed. On top of this the rough gently undulating pasture land was levelled flat, creating a proper aerodrome. More aircraft sheds were built to attract further businesses, as well as high-perimeter fencing, a formal entrance, and fenced public viewing areas within the grounds. The London Aerodrome had become a proper centre of aviation and started the next phase of its history.

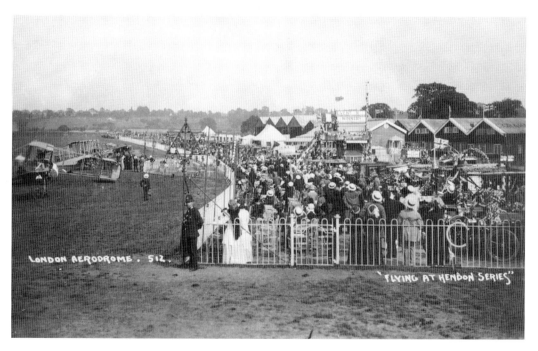

Crowds assembled in the paddocks at Hendon Aerodrome in September 1912. The star above the policeman is part of the illuminated display that took place that month. (Barnet Local Studies)

High Times at the London Aerodrome

Once the London Aerodrome had established itself as a place for flyers and aircraft makers to come to, its fame grew. It was only rivalled by the aerodrome at Brooklands, in Surrey, which had opened in 1909. However, the aerodrome at Hendon had an advantage over Brooklands: it was closer to Central London. For those who wished to investigate the wonders of flying, whether directly or indirectly, the proximity of Hendon and its aerodrome was a huge draw. In those early pre-First World War years anyone who had the

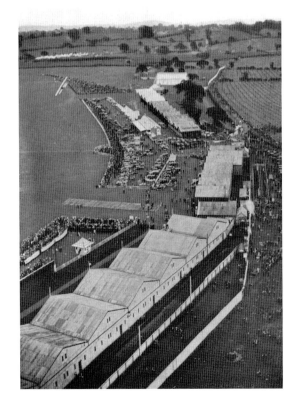

An aerial photograph of Hendon Aerodrome on a display day, c. 1912. The smoke of a Midland Railway express train can be seen in the distance, and beyond that Sunny Hill Fields and St Mary's Church, Hendon. (Barnet Local Studies)

money or the free time could indulge themselves in this new pastime. This was the 'smart set' that Claude Grahame-White understood, because he was one of them. He was adept at publicising and marketing his asset, and very soon the aerodrome was holding regular events that could be watched by ticket-buying spectators. The Aerial Derby held on 6 June 1914 attracted an audience of 75,000 people, and was attended by the Queen Mother. The events became dates in the social diaries of the well-to-do, in the same fashion as the boating regatta at Henley, tennis at Wimbledon, or horse racing at Ascot. When looking at photographs of the public flying displays, you see large numbers of motor cars parked up on the edges of the main airfield – this at a time when cars were expensive possessions to own and maintain. The majority of the vehicles were chauffeur-driven limousines that would have made the route from Central London and the Home Counties on roads that were very different from today. Such was the clamour to get to Hendon on display days, the roads nearby would see traffic jams, an occurrence familiar now, but then something entirely new. Those that couldn't get tickets into the aerodrome would find local viewpoints, and Sunny Hill Fields near St Mary's Church in Hendon provided an excellent view of the aerial activities. Always keen to create a stir, Claude Grahame-White arranged displays of night flying, the first taking place on 26 September 1912, and again people flocked to see the novelty, with both the airfield 'paddocks' and aeroplanes decorated with light bulbs.

However, despite all the fun and frivolity, there were serious activities taking place. On 9 September 1911 the first aerial post was carried by Gustav Hamel in his Bleriot, from Hendon to Windsor Castle, to celebrate the coronation of King George V. The same year

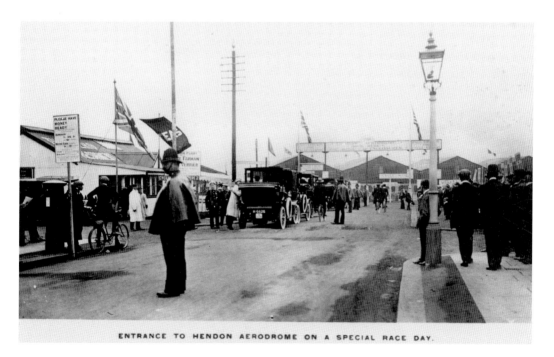

ENTRANCE TO HENDON AERODROME ON A SPECIAL RACE DAY.

Colindale Avenue leading to the entrance of the London Aerodrome, c. 1913. The turning into Booth Road is on the left past the postbox. Note the luxury limousines queuing up with their white-painted tyres. (Barnet Local Studies)

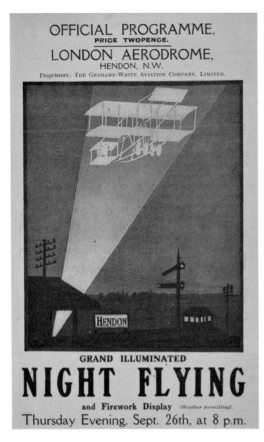

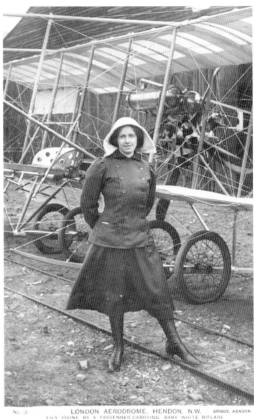

Above left: The cover to the Night Flying display programme at London Aerodrome, 26 September 1912. A certain amount of artistic licence has been made! (Barnet Local Studies)

Above right: Postcard image of Lily Irvine. The aircraft is a Grahame-White 'Baby' biplane. The rails at her feet were almost an aid to moving equipment around the aerodrome if the ground was waterlogged. (Barnet Local Studies)

also witnessed Lily Irvine become the first British woman to fly an aeroplane unaided, from British soil, at Hendon. On 23 March 1913, nineteen-year-old Marcel Desoutter, son of a French immigrant watchmaker, crashed his Gnome-Bleriot aircraft at the Easter aviation meeting. The accident left with him with a broken leg which then had to be amputated. Initially given a wooden artificial leg, his inventive brother, Charles, created an articulated leg made from Duralumin alloy metal. This solution allowed Marcel Desoutter to fly once more by May 1914. The two brothers went on to set up a company making artificial limbs at a factory in Central London. Demand for the appliances was so high during and after the First World War that Desoutter Brothers Limited were able to open a new factory at Hendon at the corner of The Hyde and Hay Lane in 1924. By this time the company had diversified into electric and pneumatic tools, which were widely used by the aircraft industry. The company moved from Hendon in the 1990s, and a car showroom is now on the site.

On 9 May 1914 William Newall made the first parachute jump in Britain, at Hendon. Sat on the port undercarriage of the Grahame-White Charabanc flown by R. H. Carr, and with the 40-lb parachute in his lap, Newall made the drop from a height of 2,000 feet, initiated by a sharp kick from the passenger, F. W. Gooden. The fall took two minutes and twenty-two seconds, with Newall landing safely in a field between Hendon and Mill Hill.

The activities at Hendon were curtailed by the commencement of the First World War in August 1914. The aerodrome became a training station for the Royal Naval Air Service and the Royal Flying Corps, as well as acting as a proving and acceptance park for new types of warplanes. Many of the new pilots learning to fly lodged at No. 7 Booth Road, including future fighter aces Albert Ball and Mick Mannock. Under the eventual control of the Royal Air Force in the interwar years the aerodrome saw a return of air shows with the annual RAF Pageants attended by thousands of spectators, many of whom arrived by London Underground trains at Colindale station. On 12 July 1921 famous aviator Harry Hawker was killed whilst he was preparing for that year's Aerial Derby. His Nieuport Goshawk burst into flames and crashed on land near Burnt Oak, and Hawker's body was found nearby. The return of world conflict in 1939 again stopped the fun and RAF Hendon was used briefly as a fighter station in the Battle of Britain, but then resumed as a transport station and a place to fly dignitaries from. In the post-war period Hendon

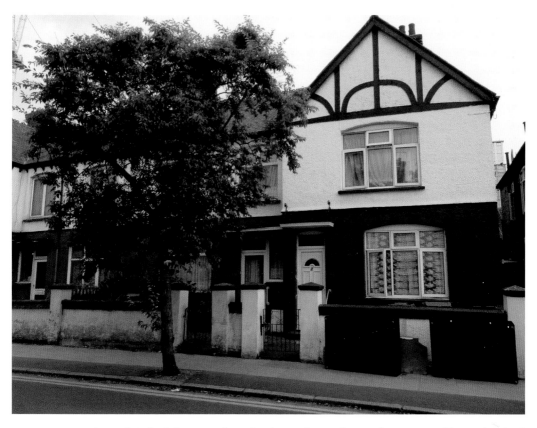

No. 7 Booth Road, Colindale, a popular pilots' guest house during the First World War. (Author)

continued as a home for communications flights, operated by both the RAF and the US Navy, for government and diplomatic work. There was not to be a return of the great interwar pageants, but instead annual 'RAF at Home' days with flypasts of military aircraft, and static displays on the airfield.

The post-war period saw the days of the operational aerodrome at Hendon coming to a gradual end. The area around the airfield was built up and pressure was building on the government to close the facility. On 4 November 1957 the remaining active unit, the Metropolitan Communications Flight, made its last sortie from the base, moving over to RAF Northolt. The runways at Hendon then sat dormant for the next decade, with occasional visiting aircraft, as well as providing a home to Air Training Corps gliders. In January 1967 a German Luftwaffe Noratlas military transport aircraft made an accidental landing at Hendon, the embarrassed pilot mistaking the airfield for RAF Northolt. The summer of 1967 witnessed the strange sight of wooden mock-ups of Second World War US C-47 transport planes for the production of the war film *The Dirty Dozen*. By this time an agreement had taken place allowing the airfield to be used for social housing by the Greater London Council – the vast expanse of levelled land was too valuable to leave empty and unused.

For many years there had been hopes to create a museum for the Royal Air Force, and by the mid-1960s a decision had been made to make the site Hendon, using the original First World War 'Belfast Truss' hangars as its core. It was a fitting choice for what had been such a historic site, and it was eventually opened by Queen Elizabeth II in November 1972. On 19 June 1968 one of the aircraft that was to be an exhibit, an RAF Transport Command Blackburn Beverley, was to be the very last RAF fixed-wing aircraft to land at Hendon. The huge four-engine aircraft was brought in with just enough space to land. A month later there was a special Founders' Day to celebrate the fiftieth anniversary of the Royal Air Force, with static displays of historic aircraft, flypasts and special guests. By this time the runways had started to be ripped up in preparation for the building of the new housing estate, given the name Grahame Park in a partial recognition of the aerodrome's founder. The very last fixed-wing aircraft to land at Hendon arrived by accident on 22 December 1968, when a trainee pilot in a civilian Piper Cherokee was forced to land due to low cloud. A second Cherokee arrived later that day with an experienced pilot to take the first aircraft away. The two aeroplanes departed the same day, marking an unceremonious end to Hendon's flying days.

The RAF remained on the East Camp side of the former aerodrome, in a collection of buildings that remained, some of them dating back to Claude Grahame-White's time. RAF Hendon remained as a supply and logistics facility until 1 April 1987. The day of its official closure was marked with great ceremony; however, a flypast of ten historic aircraft had to be cancelled because of bad weather. The RAF Puma helicopter which had been brought in to allow a TV camera crew to film the flypast ended up being the very last military aircraft to fly out from the RAF station. After the Royal Air Force's departure, the University of Middlesex took over the 1917 mock-Tudor Officers' Mess and the land around it for student accommodation. The rest of the East Camp sat neglected and derelict until the early 2000s when it was bought by a developer and has since become the vast Beaufort Park residential development.

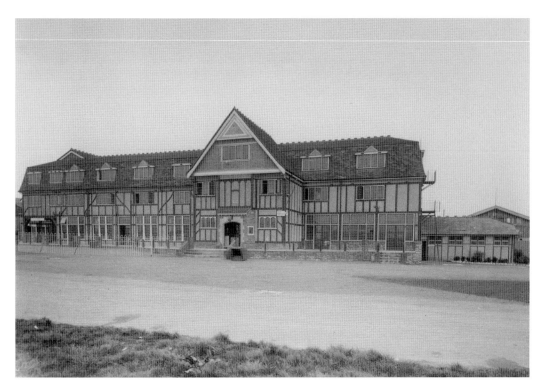

The Officers' Mess building, Hendon Aerodrome, *c.* 1920. Built by Grahame-White in 1917, with a view to being a hotel after the war. (Barnet Local Studies)

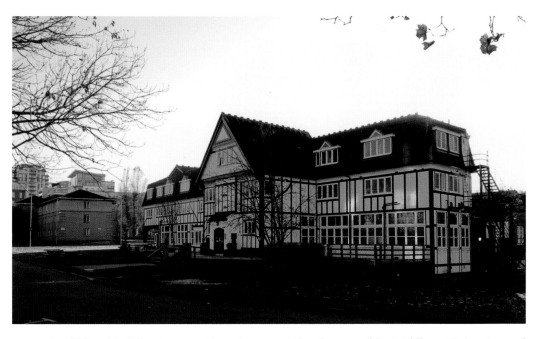

The old hotel building in 2021. Since the 1990s it has been used by Middlesex University, and was renamed Writtle House. (Author)

Aircraft Constructors along the Edgware Road

Central Aircraft Company

The woodworking firm of Richard Cattle Limited were based in a factory at No. 27 Wybert Street, NW1. Like many manufacturers they were given war contract work, and in particular they produced spars, struts and ribs for aircraft. By 1916 they merged with the Kilburn company of John Allen and Sons, forming the Central Aircraft Company. John Allen's had been a successful woodworking and housebuilding company, with offices in a large house at No. 179 Kilburn High Road, formerly known as The Elms. In the grounds of the house they had built a sizeable factory, which they had named the Palmerston Works.

Central produced parts of aircraft that would then be shipped out to the larger aircraft makers. However, by the end of the First World War the company had gained enough insight to be able to produce their own aeroplane. The Centaur IV made its first flight in 1919, from a piece of land off nearby Willesden Lane, which rather laughably became known as 'Kilburn

---

ANNOUNCEMENT!

R. CATTLE

27, Wybert St., Stanhope St., N.W.,

has pleasure in announcing that owing to large increase in his <u>Aircraft</u> business he will in future conduct same quite separately under the style of

THE CENTRAL AIRCRAFT CO.

Palmerston Works, 179, High Road, Kilburn. TELEPHONE: HAMPSTEAD 4728

1916 press advertisement for Central Aircraft. (Aviation Ancestry)

Aerodrome'. The aircraft was a basic design with a single engine and three seats. A total of eight were made and were used by the company for instructional use and joyrides, operating from Northolt Aerodrome in West London, where Central had set up its main flying base. The company did so well from joyrides that they decided to design a larger aircraft, the Centaur II. The new aircraft was able to carry six passengers within its fuselage, with the two crew in an open cockpit. Only two Centaur II's were built, and with no orders coming in Central Aircraft Company decided to call it a day in 1920. There was one further foray in 1922 when the company was commissioned to build a glider called the Sayers S.C.W.

Although Central Aircraft had created another side to the business, in the form of cyclecars (a low-cost alternative to cars, using motorcycle engines), by 1926 the company had ceased business, and returned to furniture making. The site of the offices and Palmerston Works were redeveloped into the huge Kilburn State Cinema, which opened in December 1937.

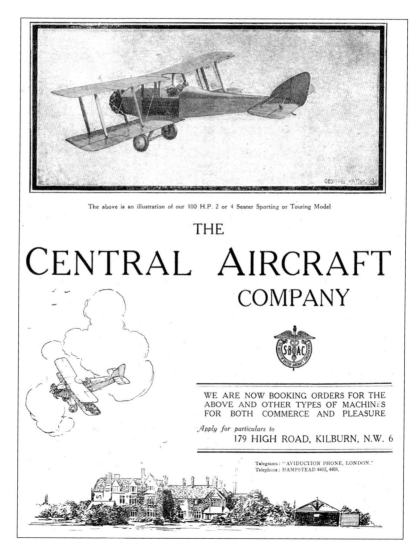

1918 press advertisement for Central Aircraft. With the war coming to an end the company was hoping for civilian orders. (Aviation Ancestry)

The above is an illustration of our 100 H.P. 2 or 4 Seater Sporting or Touring Model

THE

CENTRAL AIRCRAFT
COMPANY

WE ARE NOW BOOKING ORDERS FOR THE ABOVE AND OTHER TYPES OF MACHINES FOR BOTH COMMERCE AND PLEASURE

Apply for particulars to
179 HIGH ROAD, KILBURN, N.W. 6

Telegrams: "AVIDUCTION PHONE, LONDON."
Telephone: HAMPSTEAD 4403, 4404.

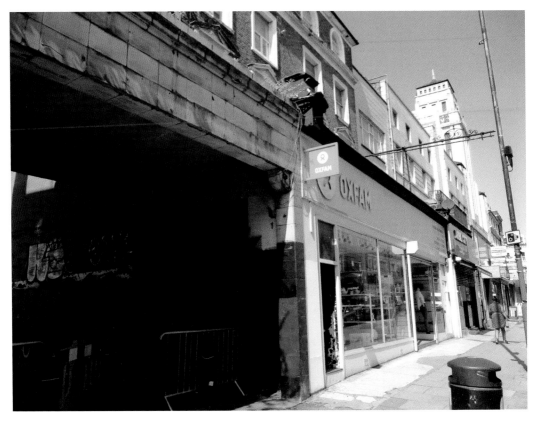

2021 view of No. 179 Kilburn High Road. The opening to the left is called 'The Terrace' and was the original way into the Palmerston Works. The tower of the mighty Kilburn State cinema can be seen to the right. (Author)

Handley Page

Handley Page was one of the great names of British aircraft manufacturing, existing for over sixty years, and became closely associated with the manufacture of large bomber aircraft and airliners.

Frederick Handley Page started his business at Woolwich in 1907, then moved to Barking the following year. In September 1912 the company moved again, this time to Cricklewood, into a former riding stables at No. 110 Cricklewood Lane, which covered 20,000 square feet. The move to Cricklewood was for a good reason. With a conflict expected soon, War Office contracts were anticipated for building the B.E.2, a reconnaissance aircraft designed by Geoffrey de Havilland, of the Royal Aircraft Factory, in Farnborough, Hampshire. The B.E.2a had been adopted as the standard aircraft for the British Army's Royal Flying Corps. Handley Page was keen to obtain a contract to build the aircraft under licence, utilising a large factory space to maximise output. However as it turned out only five aircraft were ordered. Cricklewood was most favourable for its location, just 4 miles away from the aerodrome at Colindale.

With the commencement of war in August 1914, Handley Page offered their factory and resources to the War Office and the Admiralty. The former declined, based on their

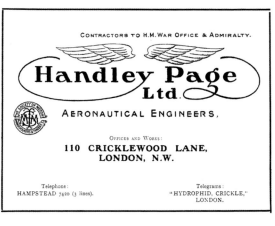

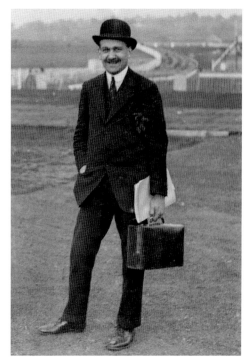

Above: 1916 press advertisement for Handley Page. (Aviation Ancestry)

Right: Frederick Handley Page at Hendon Aerodrome, 1912. (Handley Page Association Collection)

dissatisfaction with the results of the orders for B.E.2.s; however the Admiralty were keen to talk to the company about the potential for bomber aircraft. The deciding moment was when Commander Charles Rumney Samson had unsuccessfully tried to stop the German occupation of Antwerp with a small squadron of Naval aircraft. Summing up his frustration to Commodore Murray Sueter (the Director of the Air Department and founder of the Royal Naval Air Service), in a signal, Samson said 'What we need here is a bloody paralyser to stop the Hun [the German forces] in their tracks.'

This was the was the brief Sueter gave to Handley Page for what became the O/100 bomber. In February 1915 the Admiralty made an order of four aircraft, and to fund this Frederick Handley Page asked for a £20,000 advance. He took this money along to the Cricklewood branch of Barclays Bank, and asked for an overdraft of the same amount, remarking that if he were not to receive this, he would take his money to another bank. The overdraft was agreed.

Building the Handley Page O/100 prototype was to be an arduous process. The aircraft was to be fitted with two large 250 hp Rolls-Royce 'Eagle' engines, which were a development of the engine used in the Rolls-Royce Silver Ghost motor car. The combined wing and power ratio would be vital to lift the heavy aircraft and its payload of bombs to its target and back home again. As the aircraft was to be tested at the aerodrome at Hendon it would involve components being brought closer to the site from the Cricklewood factory, for final assembly. To facilitate this Handley Page was able to requisition the 40,000-square foot Thrupp and Maberly coachworks that stood on the corner of what is now Carlisle Way and the Edgware Road. The major parts of the aircraft were towed along the Edgware Road from Cricklewood by Frederick Handley Page in his Arrol-Johnston car.

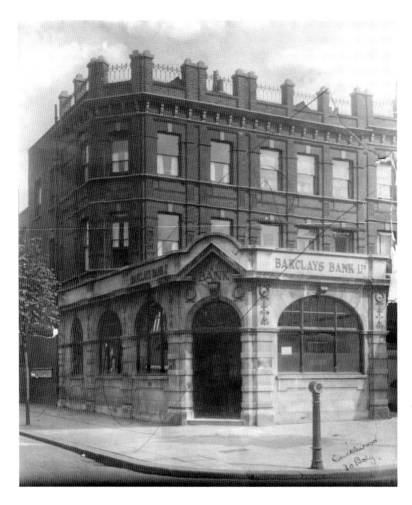

The Barclays Bank at No. 30 Cricklewood Broadway in the 1930s. (Barclays Group Archive)

For security reasons, the partially assembled prototype O/100 emerged from the building, at night, on Thursday 9 December 1915. With police creating roadblocks at the junction of Hay Lane and further up at Stag Lane, two teams of Naval ratings assisted in moving the aircraft, with its wings folded back, along the Edgware Road. Now the road is used purely by motorised traffic, but back in 1915 trams ran on rails embedded into the road surface, powered by electric current picked up from overhead wires. To ease the transit of the huge aircraft, the Admiralty had ordered that the tram wires, gas lamp standards, and telephone wires along the road be removed. On more than one occasion the tyres on the undercarriage of the plane were damaged as they caught in the tramlines. The route along Colindale Avenue was potentially full of hazards from overhanging tree branches in the gardens of homes along the route. Frederick Handley Page took things into his own hands and used a saw to cut off the offending limbs, preventing the fabric-covered body of the aircraft from being ripped. The 1.5-mile journey took an excruciating five hours. Once reassembled and all the necessary tests and checks done, the mighty Handley Page O/100 took to the sky on 17 December, piloted by Lieutenant-Commander E. W. Stedman and his co-pilot J. T. Babington.

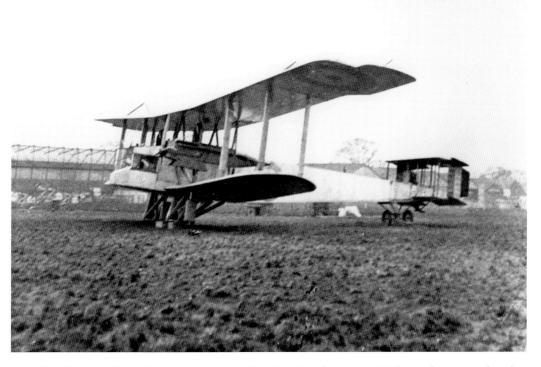

The Handley Page O/100 prototype at Hendon Aerodrome, 1916. The cockpit was glazed, a feature that was soon changed due to condensation issues. Note the carriage at the rear to ease ground handling. (Handley Page Association Collection)

Following much testing and modifications, the O/100 met the requirements of Admiralty, and the aircraft was cleared for production. At this point Handley Page became the victim of its own success, because the site at Cricklewood Lane did not have the capacity for the production numbers that would follow. A considerably larger facility would be needed, as well as an airfield. In the meantime, Handley Page sought large spaces to lease for manufacturing, with one being the ice-skating rink on Cricklewood Broadway. The company also made arrangements with other manufacturers to subcontract work out. Eventually a better solution was found not far away from Handley Page's Cricklewood Lane site. Across the lane, at the corner of Somerton Road and Claremont Road, there was a large area of open land that included Clitterhouse Farm, sports grounds and fields for horses from the nearby rest home. It had also been the home of the Beatty School of Flying, set up in 1916. The entire 46 acres of fields had been owned by the Ecclesiastical and Church Estate Commissioners of the Church of England, and were compulsorily purchased by the Ministry of Lands under the Defence of the Realm Act in 1917. Very quickly a collection of factory buildings and hangars went up on the site, erected by the Ministry of Munitions.

Having proved itself and with a total production of forty-six aircraft, the O/100 was superseded in the autumn of 1917 by the O/400, which entered service in the spring of 1918. The new version differed by having uprated engines, increasing its overall

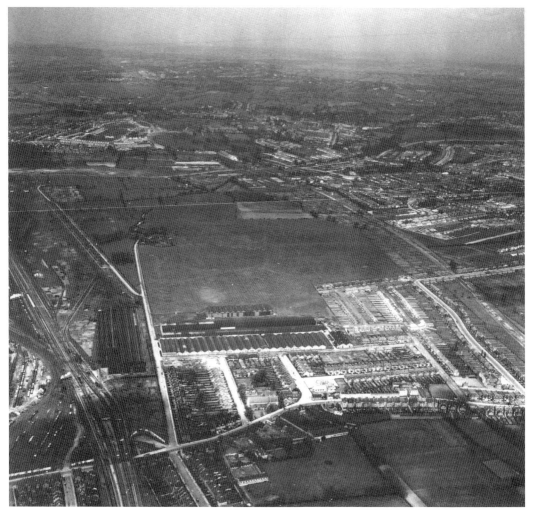

A 1931 aerial view of the Handley Page works and aerodrome. In the far distance to the left is Hendon Aerodrome. In the lower part of the image can be seen the 1912 Handley Page factory on Cricklewood Lane. (Barnet Local Studies)

performance. The ultimate version of Handley Page's Great War bombers was the V/1500. This giant aircraft was developed from the O/400 and had four Rolls-Royce Eagle VIII engines and a total wingspan of 126 feet. The bomber was designed to reach Berlin, drop its bombs and return to Britain. Given the requirement to build O/400 bombers had tied up existing manufacturing capacity, the prototype V/1500 was contracted out to the Beardmore company in Scotland and Harland & Wolff in Belfast. The completed fuselage parts were shipped from Scotland and arrived at the London Docks on 12 March 1918, then sent by barge on the Grand Union Canal, presumably up to the point where it meets the Edgware Road, at St John's Wood, and then on to Cricklewood by road. The remaining parts from Harland & Wolff were shipped across the Irish Sea from Belfast to Stranraer by steamer; they were then sent on by rail to Euston. At this point it would have made sense to transfer them onto the Midland Railway to Cricklewood; however Frederick Handley Page was keen to keep costs down and decided to pick the parts up personally, by truck, and drive them on to the factory.

Once everything was assembled and tested the V/1500 made its maiden flight from Cricklewood, piloted by Captain Vernon E. G. Busby, on 22 May 1918. Having been proven, the aircraft went into production. However, to facilitate this, work was spread out across a number of companies as well as Handley Page at Cricklewood, most notably Beardmores, Harland & Wolff, Grahame-White Aviation in Colindale, and Alliance in Acton. Despite the V/1500 being tasked to bomb Germany, the type did not get into RAF service until November 1918. The very first live mission was due to take place on 9 November, but was called off due to bad weather. The rescheduled flight was drawn up for 11 November; however this was abandoned because the Armistice was signed at midday. Although the giant bomber was never used for its intended brief, one aircraft did make the first flight from England to India in December 1918, eventually arriving the following month. The same aircraft was then used in a bombing mission on Kabul in May 1919.

With the war over, and having played its part in the overall victory, Handley Page looked forward to the future, with a particular focus on civil aviation. Much like its fellow manufacturers, the company was well aware that the conflict would come to a close, and that it needed to plan ahead. Where Handley Page had the advantage was in the size and range of its aeroplanes, and an aircraft that could reach India, in stages, carrying a bomb load could be converted into a passenger-carrying role. The first attempt was the conversion of a O/400 into His Majesty's airliner, *Silver Star*, flown by the RAF's No. 86 Communication Wing, and was used to carry delegates to the 1919 Peace Conference in Paris.

By June 1919 the company founded Handley Page Transport Ltd, starting its London to Paris service two months later, becoming the second registered British airline company (the first being George Holt Thomas's Air Transport & Travel). The company's airfield became Cricklewood Aerodrome, but because it didn't have customs for outbound aircraft, it had to pick up passengers from Hounslow Aerodrome. Fortunately, this situation was rectified in March 1920.

Using converted bombers was never going to be anything other than a stopgap, and having the confidence to see its immediate future was in civil aviation, Handley Page developed their ideas into the W.8, their first fully designed airliner. Much thought was put into the new aircraft's specifications, including wall-to-wall carpeting, circular Triplex openable passenger windows, with curtains, sixteen upholstered cane chairs, small electric candelabras, a clock, and a toilet. One cunning idea was the provision of portholes in the floor, so passengers could see landmarks as they flew over them; however this proved to be unpopular, and were later removed.

Handley Page Transport continued to be a very successful airline, and became one of the major players in this expanding market. However, by 1923 other European nations had started to eat into the market, and the British government decided that the best way forward was to merge the four British airlines into one, including Handley Page, into what became Imperial Airways.

Handley Page carried on developing new types of airliners in the following years, with perhaps its most famous, the H.P.42, making its first flight in 1930. The company continued to make military aircraft, albeit at a lower rate, with bombers being developed for both the RAF and other nations air forces. Ever the inventor, Frederick Handley Page was also

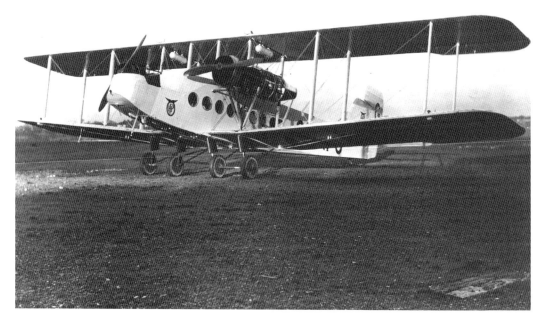

Handley Page W.8 airliner at Cricklewood. (Barnet Local Studies)

keen to develop new aeronautical design concepts. Chief amongst these developments was the slotted-wing, which allowed aircraft to reduce their stall speed, and promoted good low-speed handing qualities. Handley Page used two Airco DH9 airframes to develop the ideas, one becoming the HP.20, with a single high-mounted wing. The 'Handley Page Slot' became patented and its application in aircraft design not only improved aeronautics, it also saved countless lives. The invention earned Frederick Handley Page great personal wealth, most of which he re-invested into his aircraft business; however, he did allow himself the luxury of owning a sizeable mansion called The Limes, near Stanmore.

Handley Page will always be associated with Cricklewood, but as the company became more successful and productive it was to find difficulties with its location. Just as Handley Page was developing, so was Cricklewood and the neighbouring areas of Golders Green and Hendon, with increasing numbers of suburban homes and factories. Having a busy aerodrome located in a densely populated area was never going to be a good thing, and accidents were inevitable. The first major crash happened on 8 June 1918 when the V/1500 prototype was making its thirteenth test flight from Cricklewood, piloted by Captain Busby. Shortly after taking off, and reaching a height of around 800 feet, the aircraft's engines failed. Busby attempted to return to the airfield but stalled, and the aircraft plunged to the ground, crashing outside No. 21 Garrick Avenue, Golders Green (which at that point faced out onto open land). Only Colonel Ogilvie, who was in the tail of the aircraft, survived; the remaining five crew perished in the resulting fire. In June 2018 a memorial stone was unveiled outside the house to mark the tragic event. Two years later on 14 December 1920, a Handley Page

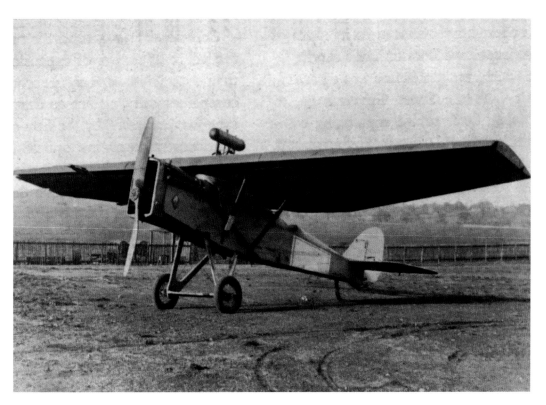

Handley Page HP.20 experimental aircraft at Cricklewood. (Barnet Local Studies)

Transport O/400 airliner bound for Le Bourget Airport in France, carrying air mail, six passengers and two crew, crashed shortly after take-off into the back of No. 6 Basing Hill, Golders Green. Four of the passengers were either thrown clear or jumped before the aircraft burst into flames. Tragically, the remaining two passengers and aircrew were killed. Despite the incident, flying continued, but by the late 1920s it was clear that with aircraft becoming larger and more powerful, the facilities at Cricklewood would not suit the company's future growth. A new airfield and assembly site was needed, and so in 1929 Handley Page opened a new airfield at Radlett, in Hertfordshire. It's worth noting that the airfield was just off the continuation of the Edgware Road, in its guise as the A5183 Watling Street.

Once the new airfield was established, the old one at Cricklewood was partially sold off for housing in the form of John Laing's Golders Green Estate, and the rest turned over for playing fields. A condition of the agreement was that no aircraft activity should take place once the land had been sold. A fence was built around the former airfield; however Handley Page was finishing work on a customer's aircraft not long before the fence went up, leaving it stranded. In an act of defiance, the company hastily erected a set of ramps and manoeuvred the aircraft up and over the fence, flying it away, all at the dead of night, with only a few curious local residents any the wiser to the nocturnal activities. The closure of the airfield did not mean the end of manufacturing at Cricklewood. The vast site continued to make large amounts of parts and partial airframes, which would then be shipped up by road or rail to Radlett for final assembly. The factory spaces at Somerton

Road continued to employ large numbers of people right through to 1965 when the site eventually closed, having outlived Sir Frederick Handley Page, who had passed away two years earlier at the age of seventy-six. The company survived until 1970, the victim of the British government's desire to rationalise the aircraft industry. Pressure had been exerted on the big companies in the early 1960s to work together, with two main players created under the names of British Aircraft Corporation (BAC) and Hawker Siddeley Aviation (HSA). Sir Frederick Handley Page had resisted this pressure, adamant that his company would stay independent; however the government favoured BAC and HSA for big military contracts, leaving Handley Page with experimental projects and civil transport. The last aircraft produced by the great company was the Jetstream, which, despite having a difficult development, went on to become a success under the eventual stewardship of BAC.

After Handley Page left the Somerton Road site, the complex of factory buildings became the Cricklewood Trading Estate and home to a multitude of businesses over the next four decades. In August 1984 a fire ripped through a large part of the site, flames leaping 100 feet into the sky and leaving a pall of smoke over north-west London. The fire destroyed a number of the former factory buildings; however business carried on until the late 1990s when the whole site was unceremoniously cleared for housing. Meanwhile, over at the first home of Handley Page, at No. 110 Cricklewood Lane, after the company departed in the First World War, the factory space was used by the Ever-Ready Razor Company in the early 1920s before they moved to Colindale the following decade. They were then followed by a refrigerator manufacturer, and in 1943 Clang Limited, an electrical equipment distributor, arrived, staying until the 1970s. In 1979 Samuelson's Film Services took over the site, turning it into The Production Village, a space for film and TV production, complete with a pub and a pond in the centre. By the turn of the millennium the whole site had been cleared and it is now a health club. On The Vale a sole Handley Page office building exists that is now used as mixed office space.

A reminder of Handley Page's presence in the area was left in the naming of Handley Grove, on a housing development of the other side of Claremont Road, actually on the site of what had been the Express Dairies depot. In March 2020 a 24-foot mural by the artist Alistair Lambert was unveiled at Cricklewood railway station, with imagery showing Handley Page aircraft.

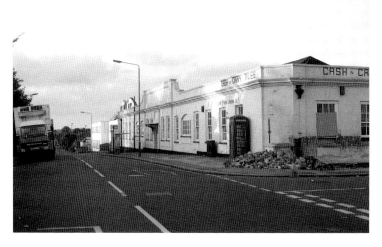

The Handley Page factory buildings on the corner of Claremont and Somerton roads, photographed in the late 1980s. (Handley Page Association Collection)

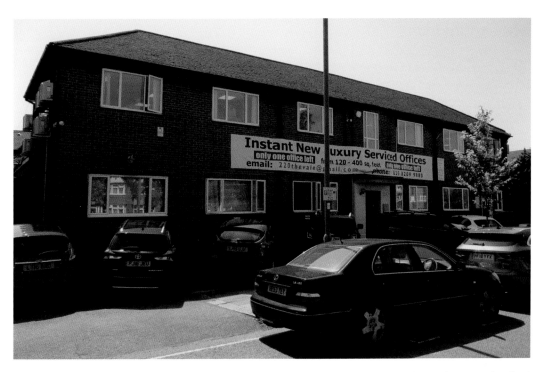

Above: The remaining Handley Page office building at No. 220 The Vale, Cricklewood, in 2021. (Author)

Below: The Alistair Lambert Handley Page mural at Cricklewood railway station, 2021. (Author)

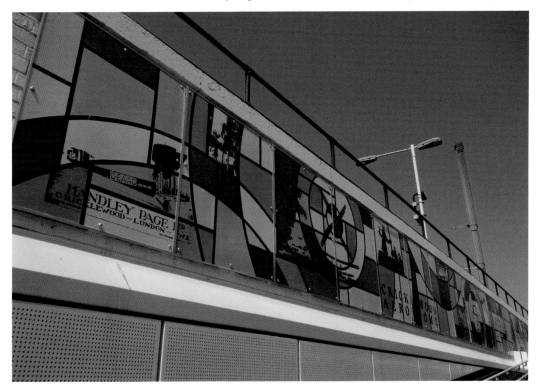

British Caudron

For many people Cricklewood will always only be associated with one aircraft manufacturer. However, there were two other companies who were within a short distance of Handley Page. Both of these companies had started off making aeroplanes of French origin, under licence.

The first of these was British Caudron, who arrived in Cricklewood in January 1915, occupying the former works of Morgan & Sharp, who made car bodies. The address was registered as No. 255 Cricklewood Broadway, although it was a sizeable concern. The company had its origins in Scotland in 1911, when thirty-two-year-old pioneer aviator William Hugh Ewen set up his flying school in Lanarkshire. Presumably aware of the goings-on at Hendon, he quickly relocated the school to the London Aerodrome and named it the Ewen Flying School. Clearly an enterprising gentleman, Ewen saw the potential of making his own aircraft and in 1912 he obtained the rights to build Caudron designs. Caudron was a French manufacturer set up in 1909 by brothers Gaston and Rene Caudron, among the earliest makers of aeroplanes in France.

With the advent of war, Ewen's flying school was instrumental in training many future pilots, and Ewen himself joined the Royal Flying Corps as a lieutenant. At this point Ewen's

Contractors to H.M. Admiralty, War Office and Foreign Governments.

The BRITISH CAUDRON
CO., LTD.
Sole Building and Selling Rights for
Caudron Aeroplanes
and Hydro - Aeroplanes
FOR
THE BRITISH EMPIRE AND DEPENDENCIES

Head Office and Works:
BROADWAY, CRICKLEWOOD, N.W.
Cable and Telegraphic Address: "CAUDROPLAN, CRICKLE, LONDON."   Phone: 5551 HAMPSTEAD

Scottish Factory and Aerodrome:
ALLOA.
Cable and Telegraphic Address: "CAUDROPLAN, ALLOA."   Phone: 52.

1917 British Caudron press advertisement. (Aviation Ancestry)

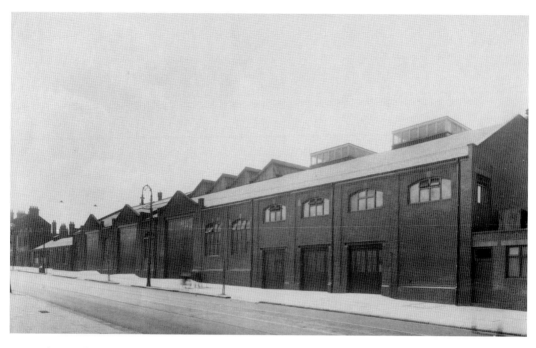

Above: The British Caudron factory on Cricklewood Broadway, *c.* 1920. Note the three huge doorways that would allow semi-assembled aircraft to exit the building. (Brent Archives)

Below: The rear of the British Caudron factory on Hassop Road, Cricklewood, *c.* 1920. (Brent Archives)

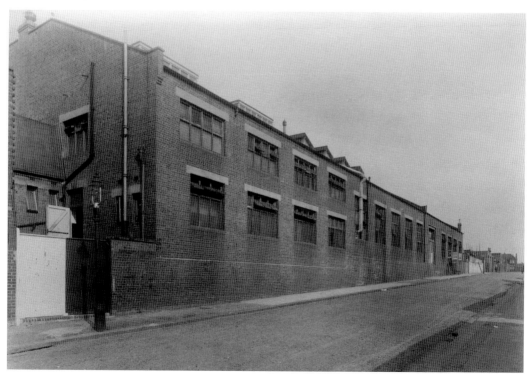

involvement with aircraft manufacturing was at odds with his military service, and the company was taken control of by Sir William Ramsey, who renamed the company The British Caudron Company Limited. The aircraft were unusual, but much liked for training and reconnaissance roles. The first successful design was the G.3, a two-seater biplane that had an incredibly short fuselage and twin booms. The pilot sat right back at the end of the fuselage, with the observer/pupil in front. The first aircraft flew in 1914, with production starting shortly after. British Caudron built 233 aircraft of this type, and you can see an example at the Royal Air Force Museum at Hendon. The G.4 followed in 1915, as a development of the G.3, and was noteworthy for being one of the very first widely used twin-engine aircraft. The type's primary role was as a bomber and was used by the Royal Navy Air Service. British Caudron built twelve examples of the G.4 – the lower numbers were down to the type being replaced by Handley Page's O/100. This development saw British Caudron becoming a conveniently located contractor to Handley Page. British Caudron shared production with the furniture makers Harris Lebus, in Tottenham, both

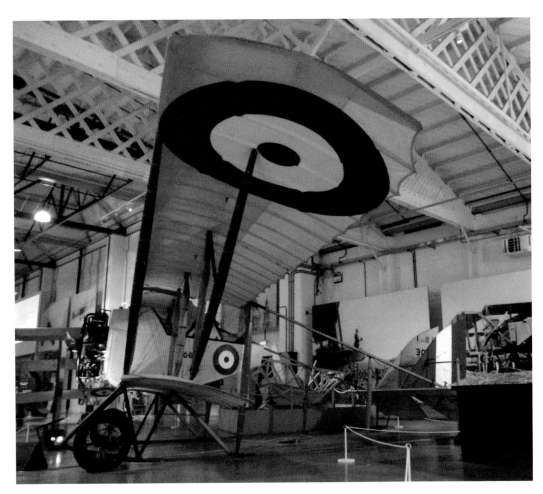

A Caudron G.3 biplane exhibited in the Grahame-White factory hangar at the Royal Air Force Museum, Hendon, in 2021. (Author)

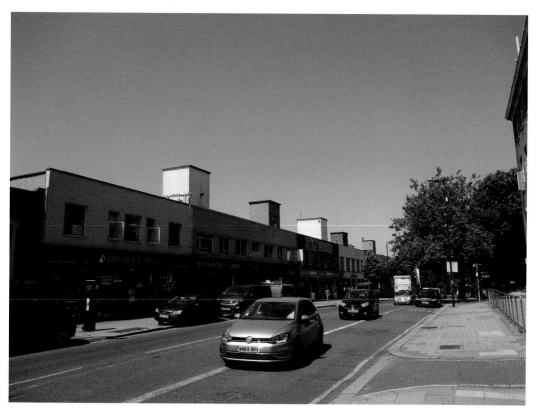

The British Caudron factory site on Cricklewood Broadway in 2021. (Author)

making the component parts for fifty Handley Page O/400 bombers. In addition to this work the company made fifty DH.5 fighters for Airco, and contributed 100 Sopwith Camels. British Caudron was exceptional in having a female test pilot, Winifred Buller, who was also the third British female pilot to obtain a flying licence – in May 1912 at the age of twenty-eight.

As with many aircraft manufacturers after the First World War, contracts for work dried up and the business closed its operations in Cricklewood not long after. By the mid-1920s the works at Cricklewood had been taken over by the Rolls-Razor company, who made a highly innovative and successful shaving system on the site through until the 1950s. In the 1960s the company took a new direction into domestic washing machines; however by 1964 it had gone bust. The buildings were eventually divided up and altered into a collection of retail businesses.

Nieuport & General Aircraft Company

The third aircraft manufacturer in Cricklewood was Nieuport and General Aircraft Company, which had its manufacturing base at Langton Road and later expanded along Temple Road, just off Cricklewood Broadway.

1918 Nieuport & General Aircraft press advertisement. (Aviation Ancestry)

Furniture and woodworking companies were quick to adapt to the needs of the war effort, especially when it came to aircraft production. One very good example was Waring and Gillow, who initially started out as S. J. Waring and Co. in 1893, before acquiring fellow makers Gillow and Co. in 1897. The company prospered in the following years, gaining contracts to fit-out luxury yachts and liners as well as notable hotels and exhibitions. The owner of the company, Samuel Waring, decided to set up two aircraft-making operations. The first was the Alliance Aircraft Company, with its manufacturing based at the company's furniture factory in Hammersmith, and its main assembly and airfield at Acton. The main products were Airco DH9s, built under licence. The second company was called Nieuport and General Aircraft, established in 1916, and used the name of its output, namely licence-built designs from the French Nieuport company. The site where the factory was located was on Langton Road, and from studying maps, most notably Stanford's map of 1872, I discovered this land was originally Lower Oxgate Farm. By 1906 the London Power Omnibus Company had built a garage for its fleet of motor buses, and it was this that eventually became the first part of the aircraft factory. The aforementioned bus company only lasted two years before going bankrupt, and so between 1908 and 1916 it was (according to a 1915 Ordnance Survey Map) a 'Motor Works'. It would seem that Samuel Waring chose these buildings because they were sizeable enough, not too far from the railway sidings at Cricklewood and the Edgware Road. Both forms of transport would allow the company to ship in materials and move out finished aircraft in disassembled sections.

British Nieuport and General started out manufacturing Nieuport 11 fighters, a well-proven design that was also being made in a number of other Allied countries, including Italy, the Netherlands and Russia. The company then moved on to produce the Nieuport 17, which was a development of the 11. However, the company only got to build fifty of the original order of 100 for the RNAS, as the design was considered obsolete almost as soon as it entered service, such was the rapid development of fighter aircraft. The company then moved on to build the Sopwith Camel, producing 300 of the legendary fighters. The acquisition of the designer Henry Folland (who had designed the S.E.5) in 1918 led to the development of the Nieuport Nighthawk. Sadly, indecisions over the engine to power it, and the end of the war, denied it the chance to prove itself and

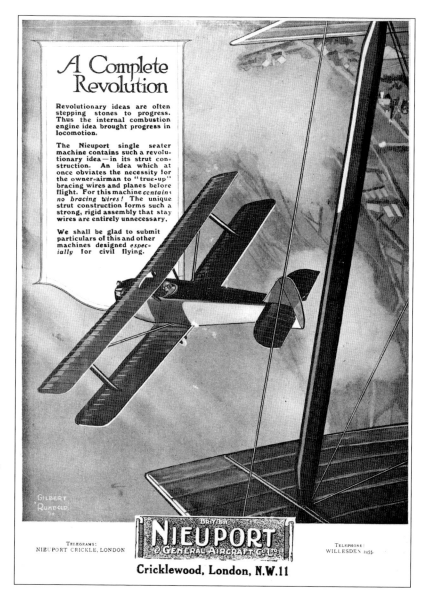

1918 magazine images of the Nieuport & General Aircraft factory on Temple Road, Cricklewood. (Graces Guide)

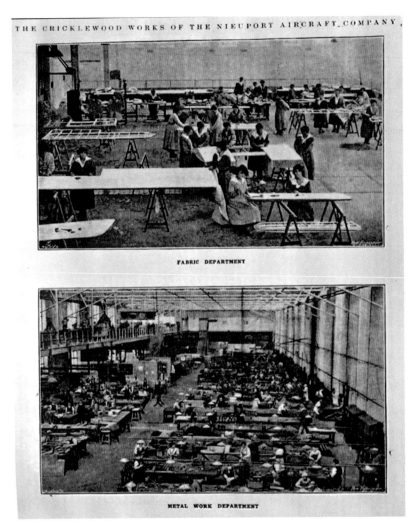

FABRIC DEPARTMENT

METAL WORK DEPARTMENT

1920 press advertisement for Nieuport & General Aircraft. (Aviation Ancestry)

production was only ever in limited numbers. A similar fate awaited another ambitious design by Folland: the Nieuport London, which was a two-engined night bomber. Again, issues with finding engines slowed its development, and only two were made and did not fly until 1920.

By 1918 the company needed more production space and a large assembly hall was built along Temple Road, which ran at 90 degrees to the existing factory space. As with other aircraft manufacturers after the First World War, slowing orders meant that Samuel Waring decided to cut his losses and closed both British Nieuport and General, as well as Alliance, in August 1920. The large building on Temple Road was of particular interest to Oswald Stoll, a theatrical entrepreneur, who had moved into film-making. Stoll purchased the building and took full advantage of the huge space inside to create at the time, he claimed, 'Britain's largest film studio'. Over the next eighteen years Stoll Studios became a home to many film productions, including some of the 'Old Mother Riley' films. Film-making in the 1930s became increasingly more difficult, especially with competition

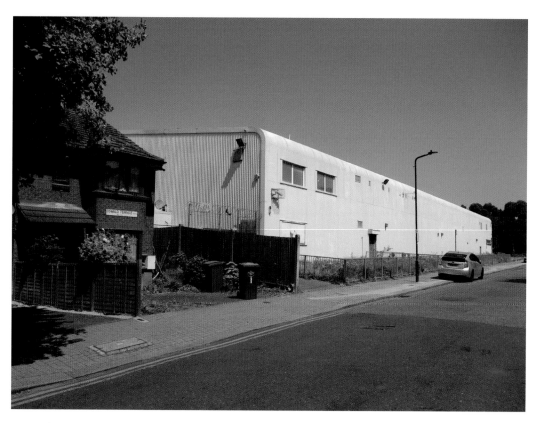

The site of the Nieuport & General Aircraft factory on Temple Road, Cricklewood, in 2021. The white building is a Matalan store. (Author)

from new American-backed studios like MGM in Borehamwood. By 1938, with the advent of war approaching, the aircraft company of Hawker Siddeley took the building over for war work, meaning it had a role in both of the major conflicts of the twentieth century. In 1948 the building was purchased by Smiths Industries, who had been operating on the site behind since 1915, producing clocks, gauges and instruments, a great deal of which had gone into aircraft. Smiths eventually wound down their activities in Cricklewood in the 1980s, and the buildings were raised to the ground, including the former British Nieuport factory. The space is now occupied by a rather inglorious steel shed, housing the clothing retailer Matalan. The old factory space on Langton Road, which had been home to a number of businesses over the years, including Smiths, has been replaced by housing.

Kingsbury Aviation

Kingsbury Green was, until the arrival of the Underground railway in 1932 and the inevitable suburban growth, a quiet rural community. Along Church Lane, before it joins Kingsbury Lane (which itself joins up with the Edgware Road a little further eastwards) was once the site of Kingsbury House. It was in the grounds of this house that Barningham Limited, a machine tool engineering company, had set up business in 1915 to make components for the war effort. By 1916 they had become involved in the manufacture of aircraft, and the need for more space forced the company to purchase the Kingsbury House estate, which covered 109 acres. They secured planning permission to build two hangars, and created an aerodrome on the land now known as Silver Jubilee Park. Barningham separated this part of their business, creating Kingsbury Aviation Company, and naming their flying ground Kingsbury Aerodrome. The company's first big contract was building 150 Airco DH.6 trainers for the RFC, followed by an order for thirty Sopwith Snipes. At the height of production, in 1918, there were 800 workers employed on the site.

The end of the war saw Kingsbury Aviation producing a stand-on motor scooter called 'The Kingsbury Scooter' which initially sold well, but then declined. There was a brief foray into light car production, but this also failed. The company went into liquidation in 1921, and the buildings were purchased by the motor car coachbuilders Vanden Plas in 1924. One of Vanden Plas' best customers was Bentley Motors, who set up a factory on the Edgware Road near Cricklewood in 1920. It was at Kingsbury where the famous Le Mans winning racing Bentleys were prepared. In the Second World War the company made parts for the de Havilland's Mosquito and Tiger Moth, then after the war, the link with de Havilland continued with the manufacture of parts for the Vampire jet fighter. The Vanden Plas works closed in November 1979, and most of the site was redeveloped as a trading estate.

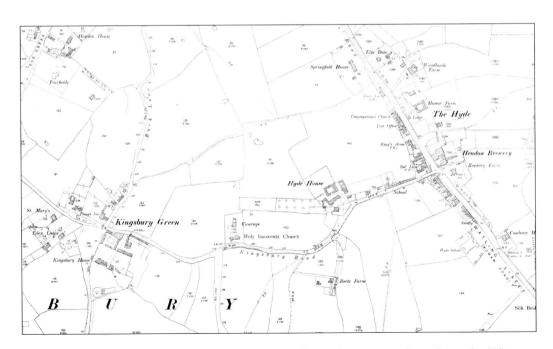

1912 Ordnance Survey map detail showing the site of Kingsbury House (just above the 'U'), where Kingsbury Aviation eventually built aircraft. The land to the right of the site was used as a small airfield. (Barnet Local Studies)

The Aircraft Manufacturing Company ('Airco')

Airco, or The Aircraft Manufacturing Company as it was formally known, was without doubt the biggest aircraft manufacturer on the Edgware Road in terms of its size and productivity. The company's owner, George Holt Thomas, played a vital part in the early days of British aviation, and despite this, his input is often forgotten. It was Holt Thomas's acquisition of Geoffrey de Havilland to become Airco's aircraft designer that made the company's products amongst the best in their class.

George Holt Thomas was born in 1869, in Stockwell, South London. His father was William Luson Thomas, who established *The Graphic* weekly newspaper the year his son was born. After George left university in 1890 he joined his father's newspaper business as a director, and later created his own title called *The Bystander* in 1903. This new tabloid magazine became very popular, and it is notable for the comic strip 'Old Bill' created by the artist Bruce Bairnsfather. Holt Thomas made his fortune from his involvement in the publishing world, and it was this money that allowed him to move into a new area of interest – aviation. In the summer of 1909, he attended the preparations for Louis Bleriot's crossing of the English Channel, and in the August of that year he attended the world's first aviation meeting at Rheims, in north-eastern France. At this event Holt Thomas was

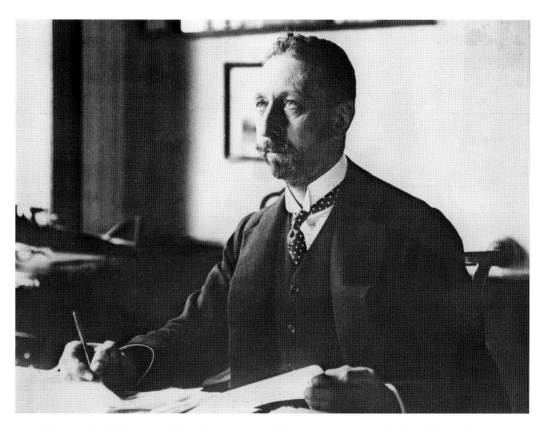

George Holt Thomas at his desk, *c.* 1919. (Royal Aeronautical Society (National Aerospace Library) /Mary Evans Picture Library)

impressed by the flying of Louis Paulhan, and took his first flight with Henry Farman. Together with his brother Maurice, Farman had made great strides in aircraft design, construction and flying. Both brothers had been born in France of English parents, their father being the Paris correspondent of the *London Evening Standard*, Thomas Frederick Farman.

Following the Rheims event, Lord Northcliffe, the influential owner of the *Daily Mail*, decided that an aviation event should be held in Britain. He chose the popular northern coastal resort of Blackpool, and George Holt Thomas became involved in the project, which started on 18 October 1909. Prizes were offered for various stunts and records, and despite the weather being poor, 200,000 people attended the five-day event. Believing that London needed to have a similar exhibition, Holt Thomas quickly persuaded the owners of the Brooklands racetrack in Surrey to clear space in the centre of the circuit, and at the end of October a three-day event took place there. As he had at Blackpool, Louis Paulhan flew his Farman aircraft, performing various stunts, including rising to a height of 977 feet.

Holt Thomas had built up a good relationship with Louis Paulhan, and he entered the Frenchman into the *Daily Mail*'s London to Manchester Air Race held in April 1910. The race was a significant event, with a prize of £10,000 to the aviator who could make it from the offices of the *Daily Mail* in London to their offices in Manchester within a twenty-four-hour limit. Looking for an operational base in London, Holt Thomas chose the field used by Kenelm Edgcumbe at the end of Colindale Avenue, and with good reason, it being close to London and having a hangar to store the aircraft. It is somewhat ironic that one of the other competitors in the race, a certain Claude Grahame-White, would end up leasing this field and turning it into the London Aerodrome. As it happened Grahame-White flew his Farman aircraft from Park Royal in West London, but in the end, it was Louis Paulhan who won the race, arriving in Manchester on 28 April, taking four hours and twelve minutes to complete the 195-mile distance. Sadly, Claude Grahame-White failed to finish, having been beset by engine problems.

George Holt Thomas enjoyed a mutually beneficial relationship with the Farman brothers and in 1911 he became the British agent for their aircraft. He looked into finding a manufacturer, but in the end realised it made more sense to do it himself, and later created the Aeroplane Supply Company to undertake the task. The first aircraft were made at Holt Thomas's other business, Airships Limited, at their factory in Merton, South London. The aircraft parts were then shipped out to the London Aerodrome at Hendon and assembled in sheds that had been previously been owned by The Aeronautical Syndicate. After a while it became clear that a full manufacturing base closer to Hendon Aerodrome would be more practical, and by 1912 Holt Thomas purchased a large brick-built garage on The Hyde at Colindale from the Metropolitan Electric Tramway and Omnibus Company. This first factory space covering 50,000 square feet would later be designated as 'Block A' by the company, and was the start of an enterprise that expanded its footprint considerably over the next six years.

On 12 June 1912, the Aeroplane Supply Company and Airships Limited were incorporated into what became The Aircraft Manufacturing Company, with the additional trade name of Airco. This is the name most often used in relation to the company, and will be the name I will use from this point. As Holt Thomas had been developing his business, he built on his contacts within the British government, and eventually became an Honorary Advisor

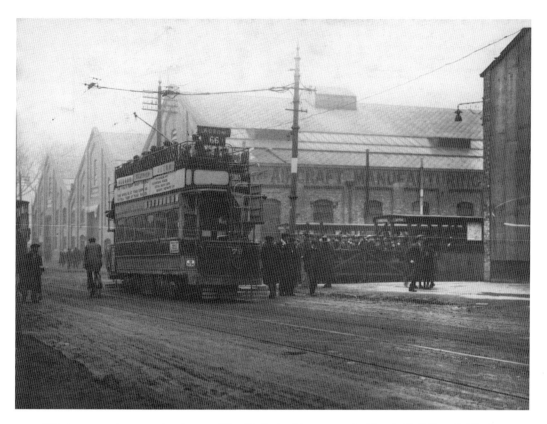

Winter 1917 photograph taken on The Hyde, looking towards Airco's 'Building A'. Workers are seen queuing on Annesley Avenue for electric trams. This one is a 66 service to Acton. (Barnet Local Studies)

to the War Office. He was keen to encourage the formation of a separate air service for the military; however this was not to occur until April 1918 with the formation of the Royal Air Force. Prior to this the British Army had created the Royal Flying Corps in May 1912, and the Royal Navy formed the Royal Naval Air Service on July 1914. By 1913 Airco had begun making Farman aircraft for the Royal Flying Corps for use as trainers, and given the potential for crashes with inexperienced flyers it meant demand would be quite high.

Until this point Holt Thomas had been buying imported rotary aero engines from the Gnome Motor Company in France. However, he was convinced that acquiring the British rights to manufacture would be a better idea long term. The firm of Peter Hooker in Walthamstow, in north-east London, were given the job of making the engines under contract. Hookers were known for making printing equipment, so yet again Holt Thomas had clearly used his contacts from the publishing world.

A vital component of any aircraft of the time was a propellor, and whilst one could be made from a single piece of wood, it was a Frenchman, Lucien Chauviere, who realised that a propellor made from several layers, or laminations, would prove a better solution. Different types of wood had certain qualities and bonding them together would make for a considerably stronger propellor. Having perfected the concept Chauviere decided to

1915 press advertisement for
the Integral Propellor Company.
(Aviation Ancestry)

set up a business making and supplying his superior solution. The company was called
The Integral Propellor Company, and had originally started out at No. 307 Euston Road
before moving to a former aircraft factory in Upper Holloway. Always keen to expand his
business, George Holt Thomas bought a share of Integral and moved the company to his
expanding works on The Hyde in 1915.

As time went on Airco had managed to acquire staff from the Royal Aircraft Factory
at Farnborough, including Hugh Burroughes, who became the General Manager, and in
1914 Holt Thomas made his shrewdest acquisition, in the form of Geoffrey de Havilland.
This talented aircraft designer had been working at Farnborough in testing and design, as
well as piloting aircraft. He felt his talents were being wasted, and on one occasion when
George Holt Thomas visited Farnborough, de Havilland made an approach. He convinced
Holt Thomas that it would be better for Airco to be manufacturing its own designs rather
than the work of others. Holt Thomas was impressed by the boldness and determination
of de Havilland and took him on initially as a test pilot in July 1914, just one month before
the war in Europe was declared.

George Holt Thomas now had all the elements required to provide the British military
with the aircraft they would need. He had the facilities and space to expand, the talents
of a great aircraft designer, and the rights to manufacture the engines and propellors that
would power these early warplanes.

The leading aviation magazine of the time, *Flight*, published a report, 'Britain's Aeronautical Industry', two months into the First World War, and described the activities at Airco under the title The Aircraft Manufacturing Company's Works at Hendon. What followed was a good description of the first factory space, later called 'Block A':

The building has three bays, each of which is of sufficient width to permit of the erection and handling of the largest machines under manufacture without undue cramping, although at present time only the centre bay is used for this purpose. To the right, on entering the building, are the metal fitting and the machine shops, which are well equipped with machine tools of various kinds, welding and brazing plants, the stores for the finished parts as well as ready use stores, and the offices for the drawing and clerical staffs. On the extreme left, near the entrance to the works, are the wood working machine shops where a large number of circular and band saw and planning machines are installed. Lower down, on the same side, are the two nacelle shops, (nacelles refer to the metal work surrounding engine areas), which are completely screened off from the rest of the building.

The article goes on to describe the good lighting of the factory space, as well as the heating systems, which were quite advanced for the time. It also mentions how the sudden increase in the workforce in these first months of the war had caused problems with housing in the nearby area, so much so that it stated 100 cottages were being built near the factory, with Airco assuring rent payments once the workers moved in. It is quite likely those homes were in Annesley Avenue and Colindale Avenue.

With Geoffrey de Havilland on board, the results of his design work started to come through, and the first aircraft to be built was the DH.1. It had been decided by Holt Thomas that all of de Havilland's designs should bear his initials as a prefix with the Airco name in front. The DH.1 was an evolution of a Farman design, having a pusher engine (at the rear behind the aircrew, and essentially *pushing* the aircraft forward, as opposed to a tractor engine, which was mounted at the front, *pulling* the aircraft). The ingenious part of the design was that the crew sat in a plywood tub, the observer sat at the front, with a gun, and the pilot sat behind and slightly higher to aid his forward vision. The design allowed the gun an unobstructed firing path, eliminating the need for the more complicated solutions that other manufacturers had come up with. The prototype DH.1 made its first flight from Hendon in January 1915. Unfortunately, it was not to be built at Airco's factory on The Hyde, as it was tied up with other work, and so production was contracted out to Savage's of King's Lynn.

By July 1915 de Havilland had designed the DH.2, which was a simple development of the DH.1, in as much as it became a single-seat fighter with the pilot taking on the role of gunner. This reduced the weight and improved performance. The DH.2 was a milestone aircraft for the Royal Flying Corps, allowing them to successfully counter the 'Fokker Scourge', a phrase given to describe the advantage the German air force had gained with their Fokker Eindecker (monoplane) fighters. A total of 453 DH.2s were built at Airco's factory at The Hyde and through other contractors.

By 1916 Airco had increased its presence along The Hyde, with new buildings going up alongside the original factory on the Hendon side (Hendon in this case referring to the

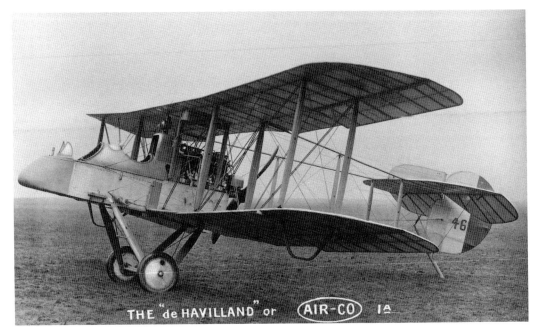

Airco DH.1 prototype photographed at Hendon, 1915. (Airco postcard from author's collection)

Borough of Hendon, which is now the London Borough of Barnet). The factory buildings were of a functional design, and quick to erect, with brick walls and steel truss roofs. The first was referred to as 'Block B' and was completed in June 1915, adding 10,000 square feet to Airco's manufacturing space. Into this new building moved the fabric and doping departments. In the section next to the corner of Colindale Avenue went the Integral Propellor division. The amount of work being handled by the company meant that a large administration building was required, and this went up on the Kingsbury side of The Hyde (now the London Borough of Brent) in the same year. This grand three-storey building, which survives as a school, was a vogueish neo-Georgian-style brick-finished structure, with a grand entrance and lobby.

The year 1916 was to see the next major Airco design arrive, that of the DH.4 (the DH.3, a twin-engine bomber, was designed but only two were built, and it was felt it lacked the performance needed). The DH.4 is considered by many First World War historians to be one of the definitive Allied warplanes of the conflict. It was a very different aircraft to the DH.2, in terms of purpose and design. The engine, by Beardmore, Halford, Pullinger (BHP) was a more conventional forward-mounted type with the pilot and observer sat well behind. The role of the aircraft was to be a light bomber but could also carry out reconnaissance work. A total of over 1,400 DH.4s were produced by both the Airco works on The Hyde and other contractors. The United States Army Air Service were so impressed with the machine that production was started in that country, with over 4,800 built.

Whilst the Hendon side of The Hyde had been heavily developed, Airco had been starting to build on the Kingsbury side, and in particular land on the former Grove Park estate. The Grove family owned land just off Stag Lane and had a farm there since the fourteenth century. In the late eighteenth century the then owners, who had clearly done well for

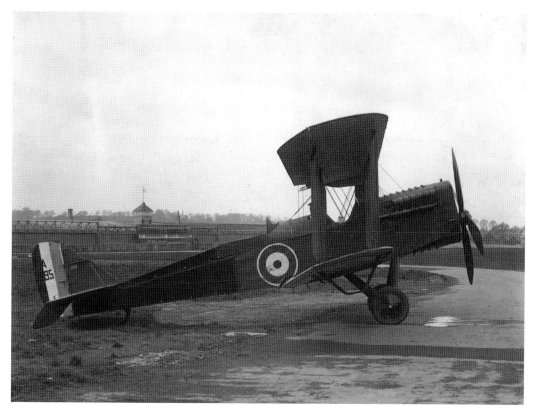

Airco DH.4 photographed at Hendon Aerodrome, c. 1916. The tower of the Grahame-White Watch Office can be seen in the distance. (Barnet Local Studies)

themselves, had an 'Adam' style mansion built, with rolling lawns that stretched down to The Hyde, bordered by trees. In June 1873 the then owner of Grove Park, John Bolton, passed away and it ended up in the hands of a property agent called Michael Walton and it was his son, William, who sold off parts of the estate to Airco from 1915 onwards. It was this land that opened up the biggest factory developments for the company over the next three years. The mansion was used for office space, and factory buildings started going up, increasing production capacity. The grounds of Grove Park had sufficient space, for not only factory buildings but also a small airfield, making it possible to fly aircraft literally straight from the factory. In most cases, they would make the very short trip to Hendon Aerodrome, where they could be assessed and passed for airworthiness.

By November 1915 the first of five bays of Block C (Grove Park Works) were built, with a further three bays added by the end of July 1916, in total adding another 2,300 square feet of space. In May 1917 Block D ('Grove Park Works Extension') and a works canteen block were completed, adding a further 150,000 square feet. This set of buildings went up on the other side of the path to Grove Park (now a road) behind the Airco administration offices. The last factory space to go up was Block G, also known as the 'Shoelands Shed', finished in the spring of 1918. Up to this point Shoelands Farm had occupied this land as well as some of the land taken up by Airco on the other side of The Hyde. Block G was a

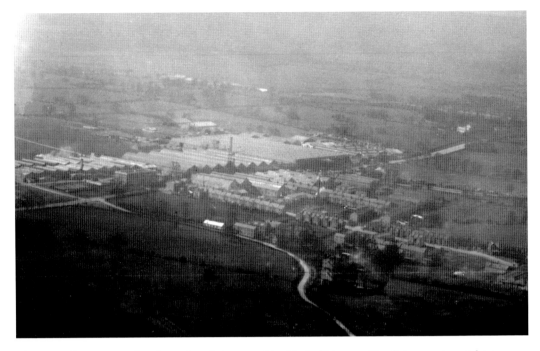

The Airco factory complex from the air in 1919. The Hyde (Edgware Road) is running right to left. The winding road in the foreground is Colindeep Lane, with Colindale Avenue to the right. The semi-rural landscape will see great changes in the next few decades. (Barnet Local Studies)

140,000-square foot main assembly hall that had been built to the latest designs, with a trussed roof that didn't require columns to support it, therefore making the production space free of obstructions. It was, in essence, a factory building ahead of its time, and would be replicated across Britain in the post-war years. Blocks E and F appear to have been the canteen blocks as seen in the plan published in a 1919 issue of the *Airco Rag*. The same issue of the magazine summed up the huge Airco complex with the following statement:

> At the time of the Armistice the total area occupied by all working sheds and offices was a grand total of 780,000 square feet, this area entitling the 'Air-Co' to call itself the largest Aircraft firm in this country, and we think in the world.

Airco would repeat the claim of being the world's biggest aircraft company in its later advertising.

In May 1918 a light railway line was opened to serve both Airco and the Grahame-White factories, taking only a month to construct. The line ran from a spur off the Midland main railway line just before what is now Aerodrome Road, running around the perimeter of Hendon Aerodrome, then through what is now Montrose Park and on to The Hyde, just opposite the 'Shoelands Shed' assembly hall. It is quite likely that the line may have crossed the Edgware Road, straight into the factory. As well as bringing in raw materials and shipping out finished products, the line was expected to carry workers, with platforms near the airfield and just before The Hyde. The Midland Railway's locos would only go as far as

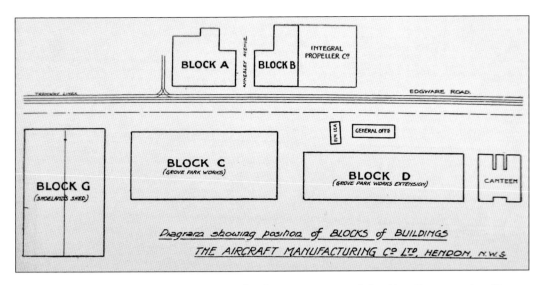

General plan of the Airco factory complex from a 1919 copy of the *Airco Rag* magazine. (Barnet Local Studies)

the first station; the rest of the line was served by smaller locomotives. A small brick-built shed was constructed to house these machines, and the building, as well as the bridge built across the Silk Stream brook, survive in Montrose Playing Fields. Although the line was rather late to make much impression for war work, it continued to be used for passengers up until 1919, and was eventually decommissioned in 1921.

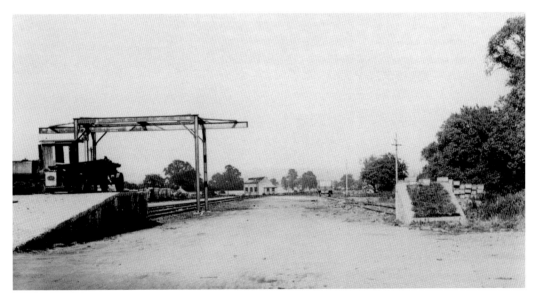

The Hendon Factory railway terminus near The Hyde, photographed *c.* 1920. In the distance can be seen the loco shed, which still exists. The trackbed in the foreground is now the Greenway. (John Alsop)

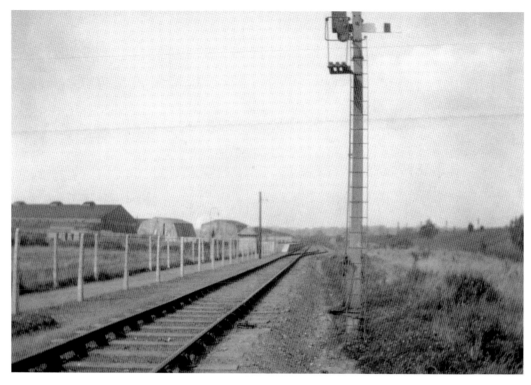

Above: The Hendon Factory railway, near Aerodrome Road, *c.* 1920. Note the aircraft hangars to the right and the platform in the distance. (John Alsop)

Below: The Hendon Factory railway locomotive shed in Montrose Playing Fields in 2021. (Author)

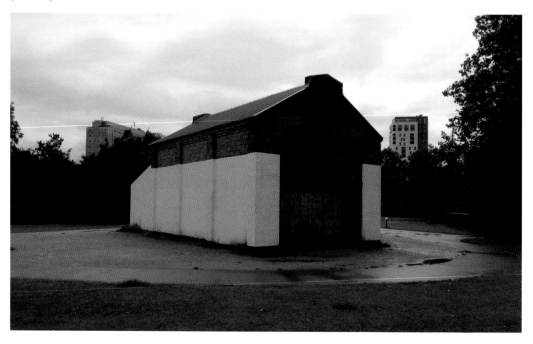

If the sheer scale of Airco's factory estate on The Hyde was impressive, so too were the numbers of people working there. By the time of the Armistice in November 1918, there were over 4,000 workers employed in various departments. Every day this huge workforce would travel in from places as far as Acton and Willesden, in most cases by tram. It was more than apparent to both Airco and the government that a solution to ease this daily migration would be to build workers' housing near the factories. As early as 1916 the Board of Works commissioned its architect, Sir Frank Baines, to design a small estate for Airco workers on a 24-acre site just off Stag Lane, opposite Grove Park. The development was to be called Roe Green Garden Village, and built to the best standards. Homes had bathrooms, cookers and water heaters, all of which were considered luxuries to many of the workers at the time. Sadly, the development wasn't finished until 1920, by which time the need had gone. Roe Green survives to this day and has been under conservation protection since the 1970s.

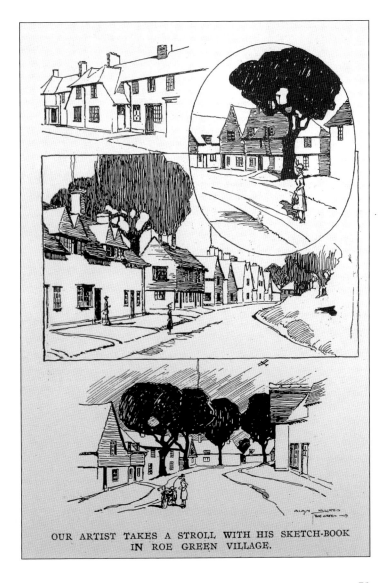

Artist's illustrations of Roe Green Village, featured in a copy of the *Airco Rag*, 1919. (Dave Scott)

OUR ARTIST TAKES A STROLL WITH HIS SKETCH-BOOK IN ROE GREEN VILLAGE.

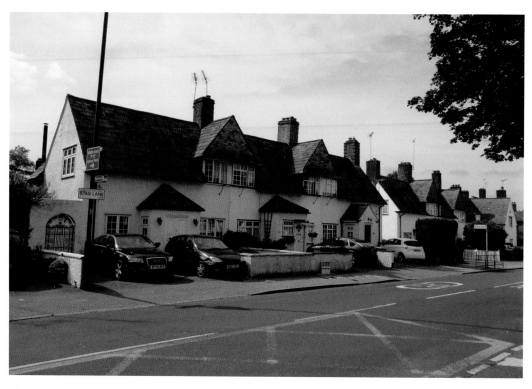

Above: Roe Green homes on Stag Lane, 2021. (Author)

Below: Goldsmith Lane, Roe Green Village, 2021. (Author)

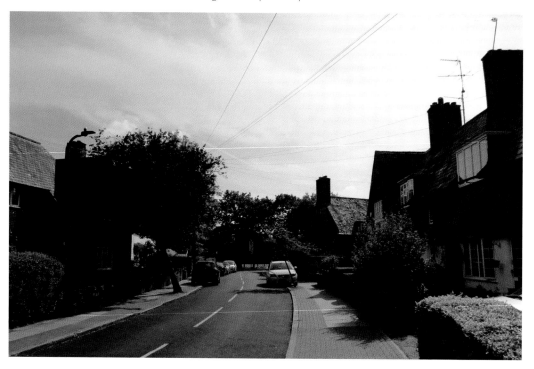

George Holt Thomas and his team were keen to ensure the vast army of workers at Airco were kept in good spirits. The daily grind of work, as well as the ongoing stress of war, meant it was vital to keep up the workers' morale. A fully equipped staff welfare department was set up to assist with health and well-being needs. Organised social activities were encouraged, sports days were held on the former Grove Park lawns, there was an orchestra, a theatre group, and my favourite, the 'Airco-medians', to provide entertainment. All of this was reported in the *Airco Rag*, a company-approved monthly publication put together by staff and acting as an outlet for workers to express their views, often with great humour. In many ways Holt Thomas and his managers had overseen what could be seen as the prototypical 'modern' production facility, with vast manufacturing halls, operating production line processes, employing equal numbers of men and women, and providing social and welfare solutions to its workforce. What had been achieved at The Hyde would become the norm in the post-war years across the nation.

At the end of May 1917 King George V and Queen Mary visited the Airco works, with the hundreds of workers assembled to greet them. The royal couple were shown around the various departments and were given a display by the company test pilot, Captain B. C. Hucks. This remarkable pilot was already a veteran of pioneer aviation, having gained his Royal Aero Club certificate in 1911, and was the first British pilot to perform a loop in his Bleriot at Hendon in 1913. Benny Hucks had joined the RFC in 1914, flying on the Western Front. Unfortunately, he had suffered from pleurisy and had to return home. His other great achievement was inventing the 'Hucks Starter'. This adaption of a Ford Model T car allowed an aircraft engine to by started by the application of a chain-powered shaft linked to the car's drivetrain. The useful device meant aircrew did not have to be used in the often inefficient and dangerous process of hand-starting the engine. The Hucks Starter was initially made by Airco and became widely used across the world throughout the immediate post-war years. Sadly, Hucks himself was not to see the end of the war, dying on 7 November 1918 from double pneumonia.

Airco, and its talented designer, Geoffrey de Havilland, developed and built a line of aircraft designs following on from the DH.4; some were more successful than others. The DH.9, introduced into service in November 1917, was supposed to be a great step forward in terms of its payload capacity; however it underperformed and losses were great. It was only when the American-designed Liberty engine was fitted that performance was improved, and in the years after the war the DH9A became a workhorse of the Royal Air Force. In March 1918 the twin-engined DH.10 bomber took its first flight. Hopes were great, but by the time the aircraft had a chance to prove itself the war was over.

Whilst the Airco complex at The Hyde was a major producer of military aircraft (George Holt Thomas had mentioned that a complete airframe was leaving the facility every forty-five minutes in the 5 January 1929 copy of *The Times*), it was not the only source of Airco machines, with many sub-contractors across Britain, such as Westland in Somerset, producing thousands more aircraft. The DH9A exhibited at the RAF Museum in London was made by Westlands. Even before the First World War came to an end, George Holt Thomas had his eyes focused on the future of flying, and in particular civil aviation. With its dominance in the provision of military aircraft, he had confidently expected to do the same in the civil market. That confidence and air of permanence was expressed in the Airco administration building on The Hyde, with its impressive entrance lobby fitted out

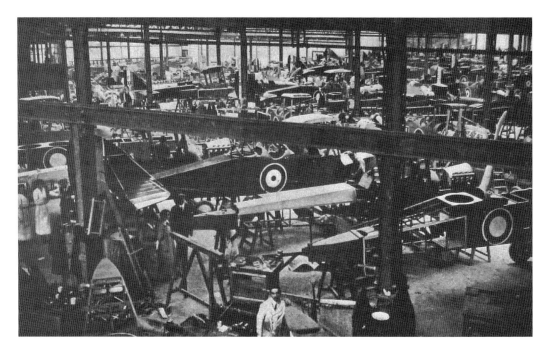

Inside one of the assembly halls at Airco, *c.* 1918. (Dave Scott)

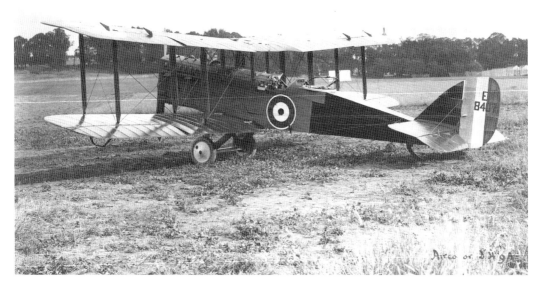

Airco DH.9 photographed in Grove Park at the rear of Block C, 1918. E8407 was one of a batch of 400 made at The Hyde. (Barnet Local Studies)

with black marble columns, carved wood and plaster decoration. Holt Thomas had already registered a company called Air Transport and Travel (AT&T) on 5 October 1916. Before the war had even finished, work had started adapting existing Airco aircraft like the DH.4 into passenger carriers, and in July 1919 AT&T made its first flights from Hendon to Le Bourget in France. By the August of that year regular flights started from Hounslow Heath in West London using the DH.16, which was a redesigned DH.9 capable of carrying four passengers and a pilot.

Unfortunately, despite George Holt Thomas's forward thinking, and Geoffrey de Havilland's designing skills, The Aircraft Manufacturing Company was heading for trouble. The end of the war had unsurprisingly meant a total lack of demand for new military aircraft, and when a company goes from producing a finished aircraft every forty-five minutes to no orders almost overnight, it was bound to cause problems. To underline the situation, it is worth considering the loss rate of aircraft dropped dramatically too, and the RAF was left with more aircraft than it had use for, leading to vast numbers being scrapped. With such large facilities and workforce, as well as suppliers and sub-contractors to pay, it was inevitable Airco would start losing money. From October to December 1919, the company had made a loss of £620,000, and at this point the receivers were called in. The British government were unwilling to come to the company's assistance, and in the end Holt Thomas had no other option than to find a potential buyer. He had already approached the Birmingham Small Arms Company (BSA) in early 1919, but at the time they felt the company's stock was overvalued. However, talks resumed in November of that year and by February 1920 BSA had taken over Airco, with Holt Thomas given a position on the board of directors, and an agreement to retain the Airco name. Not long after the deal had been done BSA realised the true depth of Airco's financial losses were much greater than they had been made to believe, and as a result Holt Thomas was forced to step down as a director. It was a sad finish for a man who had put so much of himself into British aviation development, manufacturing methods, and the war effort.

Realising they had purchased a liability, Birmingham Small Arms sought to liquidate all the assets of Airco, including the factory buildings. These large structures would eventually find new uses for all manner of manufacture over the following decades. Air Transport and Travel carried on under BSA's Daimler car hire division until November 1920, when it was liquidated. Meanwhile the workforce was left to an uncertain future, but many would return to new industries once the economy recovered. As a later section will explain, Geoffrey de Havilland was able to set up a new aircraft company with Holt Thomas's financial assistance. George Holt Thomas, however, withdrew from the aviation world, returning to his home in Buckinghamshire where he took up breeding Friesian dairy cattle. Sadly by 1926 he was affected by ill health, and he died following surgery, in Nice, France, on 1 January 1929. He was just sixty years old.

The complex of Airco buildings were eventually turned over to new uses in the post-First World War period. The government was keen that the factory spaces and their wartime workforce should not be left idle, after all, in most cases it was public money that paid for the construction of many of the buildings, under the Ministry of Munitions. The old administration building was taken over by Kingsbury County School in 1925, followed by Kingsbury Secondary School in 1932, and in 1952 it became an annexe to Kilburn Polytechnic. It is currently the Beis Yaakov School. The array of factory buildings

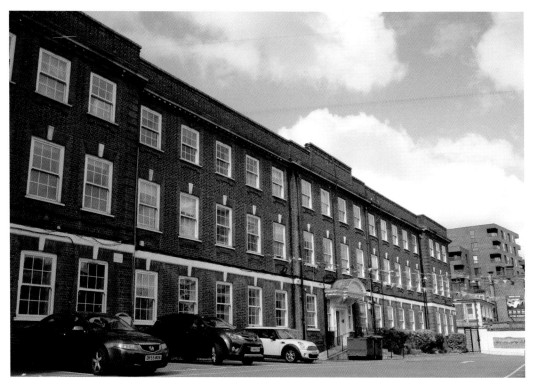

Above: The Airco administration building (now the Beis Yaakov Primary School) in 2021. (Author)

Below: The entrance foyer of the Airco admin building in 2021. Note the black marble columns. (Author)

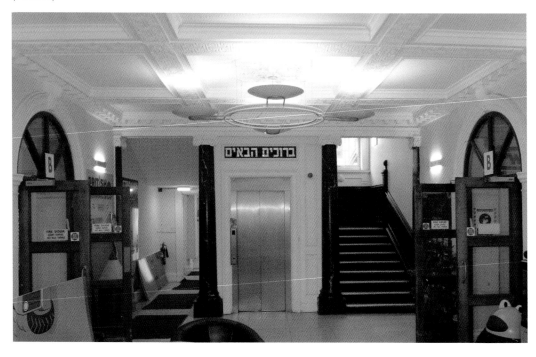

behind the admin building (Block D) was for many years home to Beardmore Motors and Windovers Ltd, a motor vehicle coachbuilder, and is now Colindale Retail Park and the Silverworks residential complex.

The set of buildings called Block C became home to the Daimler car company (which was part of BSA) and the Phoenix Telephone and Electric Works in the early 1920s. Phoenix had been in Cricklewood Lane since 1912, just down from Handley Page, and during the First World War had become the War Department signal factory, employing 1,600 workers at its height. As well as making telephone equipment, the company had an interesting sideline in the form of tinsel manufacturing, as a by-product. The company went through a number of different mergers, eventually ending up as a British Telecom site in the 1980s. The factory buildings were then cleared and a Japanese retail development called Yaohan Plaza opened in the early 1990s. This in turn had its day, changing its name to Oriental City, eventually closing around 2010. The site then sat semi-derelict until it was redeveloped yet again with a Morrisons superstore, an East Asian restaurant and supermarket, plus a residential complex opening up from 2016 onwards. A charming Airco-era relic survives at the corner of Grove Park and The Hyde, in the form of a electricity substation built in the same style as the admin building. Moving along to Block G, or the 'Shoelands Shed', and after Airco wound down both this building and the

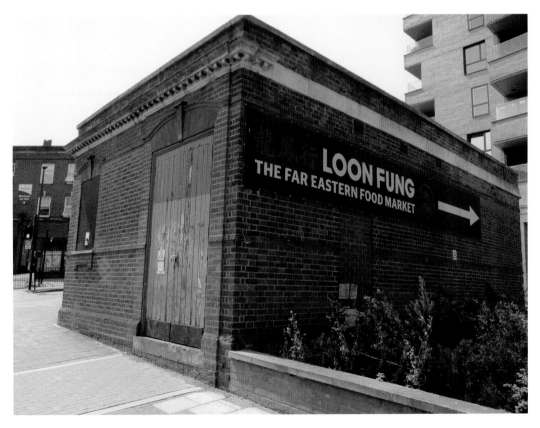

Power supply building erected for Airco on The Hyde, in 2021. (Author)

old Thrupp and Maberly factory next door were used as the 'No.1 Aircraft Salvage Depot'. Here surplus warplanes were repaired for reuse or potential sale to the open market. By 1922 this operation had ceased, and the Thrupp and Maberly works was purchased by Lamson Paragon, a paper goods manufacturer. By 1959 the company had moved out and Hupfield and Hedges, a plastics maker, moved in. The building was demolished in the late 1970s and is currently a Mercedes-Benz car showrooms. The Shoelands Shed was bought by the American vehicle manufacturer General Motors in 1923, and here the company assembled their Chevrolet trucks from kits of parts shipped over from Canada. This practice avoided the heavy importation tax on finished vehicles and was undertaken by a number of American companies in the 1920s, including Chrysler in Kew and Hudson in Chiswick. GM found the old Airco factory ideal for large-scale production work and continuous line manufacturing could be undertaken without many floor obstructions. By 1928 GM had turned over some of the factory space to its Frigidaire products (having started on Aerodrome Road a few years previously), and in 1929 truck manufacturing was moved over to a new plant at Luton, in Bedfordshire, under the Bedford name. From this point onwards the factory continued to make Frigidaire refrigerators and air-conditioning equipment right through to the late 1970s when it closed. The buildings were demolished in the 1980s and the site is now occupied by an Asda superstore, Capitol Way trading estate and the TNQ residential complex.

Moving to the other side of the Edgware Road, the original Airco factory, or Block A, had many uses after the company's departure, in particular the Safetex company who made safety glass, and by the 1950s the London service depot for Armstrong Siddeley cars. By the 1980s the site had been cleared and is currently occupied by a Boots

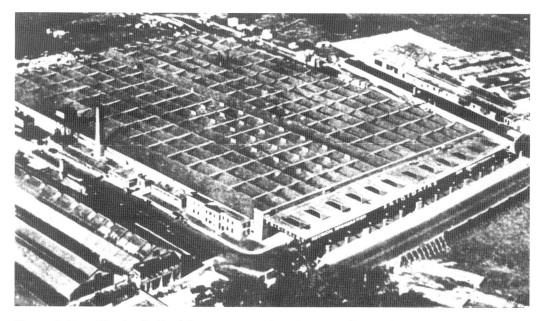

The 1918 Airco 'Shoelands Shed' factory, pictured in the 1920s (but updated in the 1930s to include the Frigidaire name). The Hendon Factory railway terminus can be seen in the bottom of the image. (Barnet Local Studies)

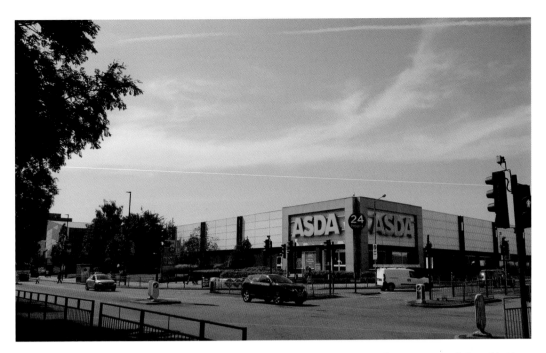

Above: The Asda superstore built in the 1980s that now sits on the majority of the old Airco 'Shoelands Shed' site. (Author)

Below: The Hyde in 1962. Airco's former factories are on both sides of the road – the building to the far left is Block A, and to its right Block B (now used by Kwik Fit). The 266 bus is the descendant of the old 66 tram service seen in the 1917 image. (Geoff Plumb)

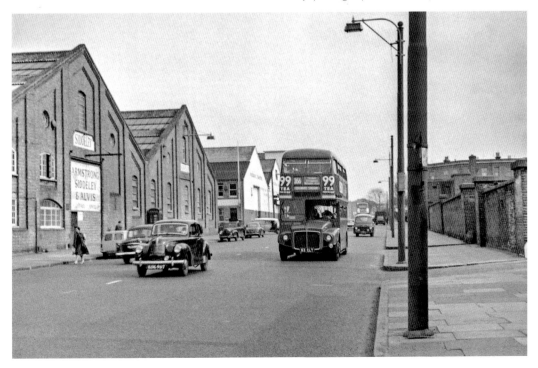

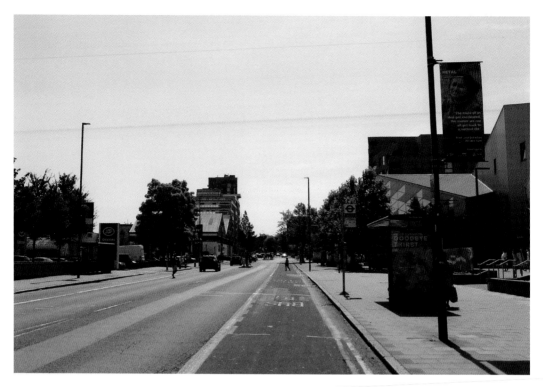

The Hyde in 2021. Airco's Block A has gone and been replaced by a Boots Opticians and a KFC. Block B can just be made out in the distance. (Author)

Opticians and a KFC drive-through restaurant. On the other side of Annesley Avenue is the sole remaining Airco factory space, part of Block B. This remarkable survivor went through many owners after the First World War, with T. F. Bristow & Co., the soap and beauty products maker, being one of the other longest occupants from the 1930s through to the 1950s. By the early 1970s the building was being used by Kwik Fit, the tyre and exhaust fitters, who remain there to this day. The original brick walls and steel roof trusses can still be seen, and although the building has been truncated at the rear, a new roadway, Mannock Close, acts as a reminder to its aviation connection. Mick Mannock was a First World War RFC fighter ace who received his training as a pilot at Hendon Aerodrome.

The site next to Kwik Fit, which had been the home to The Integral Propellor Company, had a long life with many uses after the First World War. One of the first occupants was Bandmaster Gramophones, in the early 1920s. I have also seen a reference to a piano maker, but that has been harder to pin down. By the 1930s the machine tool company of E. H. Jones had taken the building over and in the late 1930s had remodelled the front of the building to give it a more modern appearance. In the 1970s the DIY retailer Texas Homecare was using the building, and its last occupant was a children's recreation centre called 'Kid Stop'. A fire in the late 1990s destroyed the building and by the early 2000s a residential complex had been built on the site.

Aircraft factory works packed into a motor lorry, and old cart, towed behind it, next to an electric tram on The Hyde in winter 1917. Airco's Block B is in the background. (Barnet Local Studies)

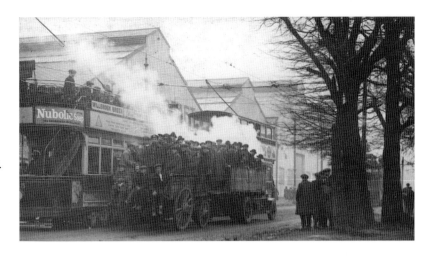

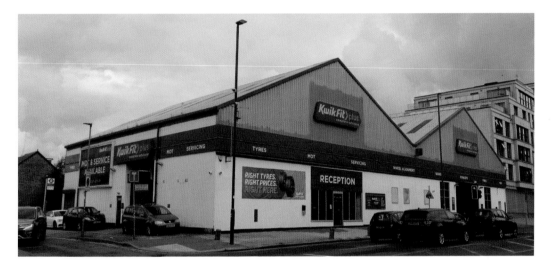

Above: The remaining section of Airco's Block B in 2021. It has been a Kwik Fit since the mid-1970s. (Author)

Right: The interior of Block B in 2021. (Author, with thanks to Kwik Fit)

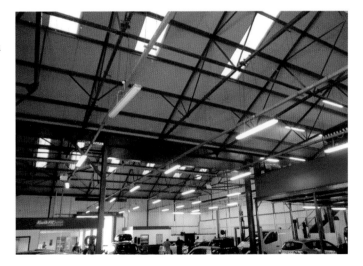

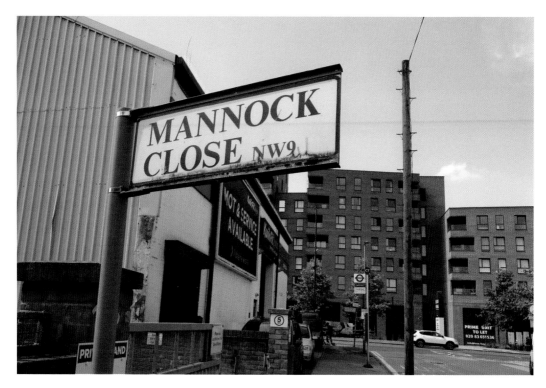

Mannock Close, a relatively recent addition, which recalls the First World War fighter ace. This is just behind Block B.

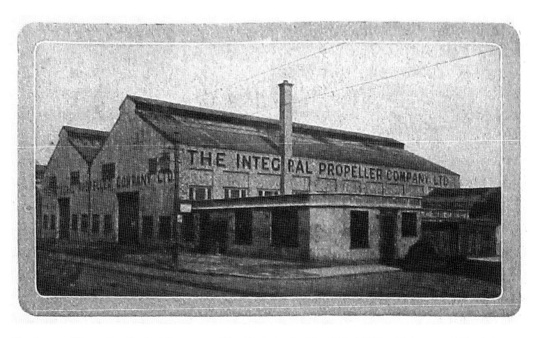

The Integral Propellor Co. Ltd factory on The Hyde in the First World War. This part of Block B is now covered by an apartment block. (Dave Scott)

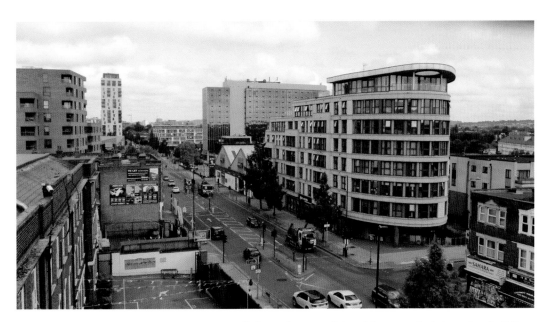

2021 view of The Hyde (Edgware Road) from the top of the old Airco administration building. Block B (Kwik Fit) is visible in the middle of the image. (Author, with thanks to Beis Yaakov School)

Grahame-White Aviation

Claude Grahame-White was, without doubt, a key individual in the creation of the London Aerodrome at Hendon, turning it from a rudimentary airfield into a proper facility where pioneer aircraft makers and pilots, as well as members of the public, could gather. It was therefore not surprising that Grahame-White was keen to be heavily involved in aeroplane manufacture. By the end of the First World War, Grahame-White Aviation Company Limited was considered as a major contributor to the British military aircraft industry, although the company's strength lay in the making of other companies' designs under contract. As well as its factory buildings and offices at the London Aerodrome, the company also used land on the other side of what became Aerodrome Road.

Before the war had started Grahame-White Aviation had built aircraft of its own designs, such as the Type 10 Charabanc, which could carry up to seven passengers for joyrides around the aerodrome and local area. Such craft were created by the designer John Dudley North, who had joined the company in 1912 at the age of twenty. Claude Grahame-White had managed to influence government and War Office officials before the First World War had begun, and just as George Holt Thomas of Airco had been, he was a keen advocate for aircraft to be used by the British military. In 1912, sponsored by the *Daily Mail*, he had flown a Farman aircraft with floats and a two-seater cockpit with the slogan 'Wake Up England' painted on the side around the country to make people aware of the threat that aerial bombardment could have in future conflicts. What may have appeared as innocent showmanship was a grim portent of what was to happen a few years later.

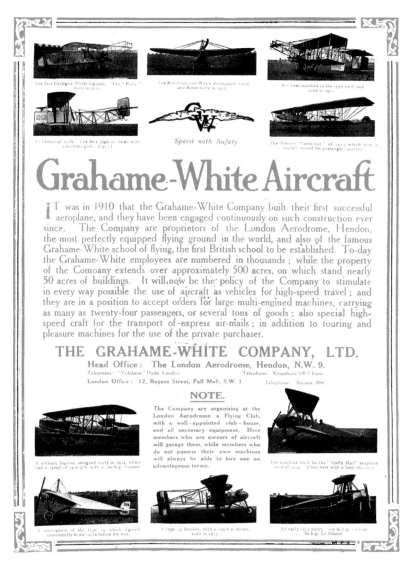

In 1913 Grahame-White had secured the rights to manufacture the French Morane Saulnier monoplanes, which proved to be popular with the Royal Navy, who ordered fifteen from the company. The start of the First World War saw Grahame-White offer his aerodrome and manufacturing capabilities at Hendon to the Admiralty. He was well acquainted with the First Lord of the Admiralty, Winston Churchill, and wanted to do 'his bit' for the nation. He also offered his services to the newly formed Royal Naval Air Service, and was duly made a flight commander. In his position as a military pilot he saw active duty, most notably making the first night-time patrol of London in September 1914, and taking part on a raid on the Belgian coast in February 1915. However his service career ended in July 1915 to allow him more time to manage his company's affairs.

Claude Grahame-White was keen to oversee the development of his company's buildings, and to some degree there appears to be an old-fashioned Victorian sensibility to his outlook. He clearly felt that there should be some permanence to the structures and that he was leaving a legacy. A very good example of this was the Watch Office building, which was erected in 1915. The style of architecture was neo-Georgian, which perhaps didn't reflect the modern, forward-looking ethos of the company's owner. However, it did give an air of established elegance, which would have allowed the public to accept the brave new world of aviation taking place at the aerodrome with more ease. The ground-floor rear exit opened out onto the airfield. On the upper floor was Claude Grahame-White's personal office, fitted out to his tastes and looking very much like a hunting lodge, with wood panelling and a handsome-looking stone fireplace. A set of grand windows and doors led out to a balcony, where the owner could overlook the airfield and entertain guests. The war would have been an obstacle to Grahame-White's ambitions to have his London Aerodrome at the centre of civil aviation, in effect a 'London Air Port'. This clearly was not to be, and London's first airport was in Croydon, before the honour went to Heathrow after the Second World War. On top of the first floor was the small lookout tower, which could probably only accommodate a very small number of people. Some consider this structure to be the world's first control tower, and certainly it was used for this task when the Royal Air Force took over the airfield, right up until flying ceased in 1957. The Watch Office building also contained a boardroom, the accounts department and drawing offices. Following on from this was a spinal block that would become factory space, leading to an entrance frontage onto Aerodrome Road. This would be where the company would receive visiting guests and officials, and the first thing they would have seen would be a large control board with electricity gauges showing the power usage of all the individual elements of the Grahame-White Company. This wonderful piece of showmanship survives at the RAF Museum, Hendon.

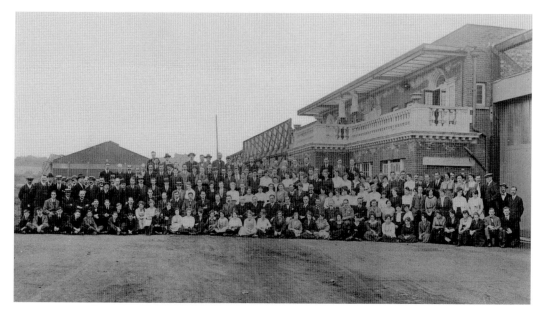

Staff and workers of the Grahame-White Company assembled on the airfield at Hendon in front of the Watch Office building, *c*. 1919. (Barnet Local Studies)

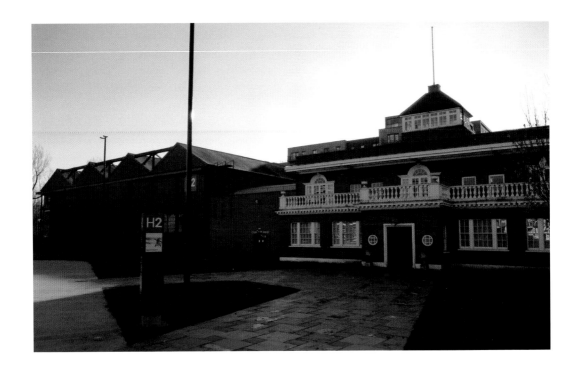

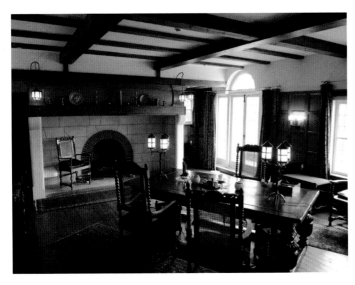

Above: The Grahame-White factory hangar and Watch Office in their reassembled positions at the Royal Air Force Museum, Hendon, in 2021. (Author)

Left: Claude Grahame-White's office in the first floor of the Watch Office in 2021. Everything in the room was carefully recreated from photographs in 2009/10. Note the monogram above the fireplace. (Author)

The Watch Office, the adjoining spinal block and entrance building were left to fall into a state of decline after the departure of the Royal Air Force from Hendon in the late 1980s. Together with some of the other historic buildings they sat gradually rotting on the derelict East Camp site. For many years the whole area was in the sights of developers, and in the early 2000s one such developer, St George, were given the go-ahead to turn the site over to a high-density housing development called 'Beaufort Park'. As part of the permission to proceed, St George's agreed to deconstruct and rebuild two of the buildings.

The Watch Office, a section of the spinal factory building and entrance frontage was moved over in 2010.

The Watch Office building was just one small part of the Grahame-White Aviation complex, and much like all the other aircraft manufacturers, as the First World War progressed, so did the number of factory buildings. As well as the existing hangars on the aerodrome, factory buildings grew up on both sides of Aerodrome Road, which had been made into a proper metalled road in the early years of the conflict by German prisoners of war. One noteworthy factory building was erected in 1918, specifically to deal with the contract to build Handley Page V/1500 bombers. This huge aircraft was the last of Handley Page's First World War heavy bombers, and Grahame-White Aviation was just one of a number of contractors brought in to build the machine. The contract was for forty aircraft, but in the end the order fell through with the cessation of the war. The Grahame-White Factory Hangar, as it is referred to now, was built to the most modern standards, covered by a steel-truss roof, with two floors of offices overlooking the production space and huge sliding doors out onto the airfield. This structure was the first of the two buildings deconstructed and moved over to the RAF Museum site by developers St George in 2003. It now houses the museum's collection of First World War aircraft.

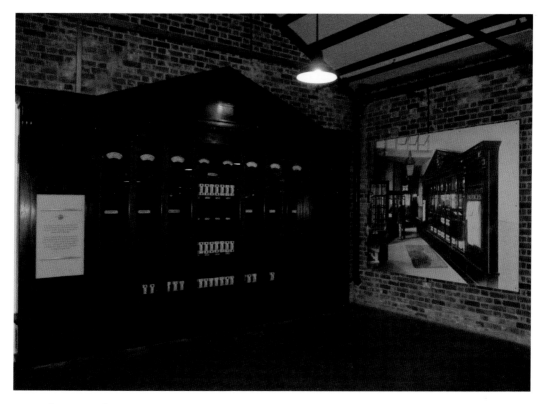

The original Grahame-White factory electrical display cabinet, displayed at the RAF Museum, 2021. An enlarged photographic image of the cabinet in the First World War is alongside. (Author)

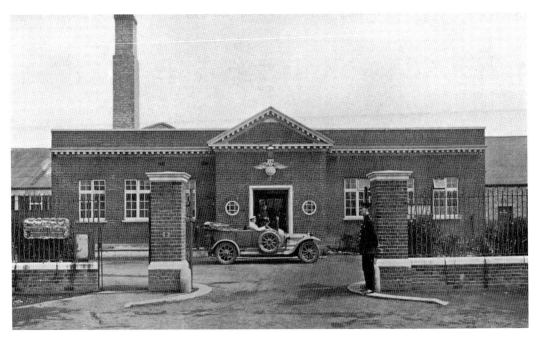

The Aerodrome Road entrance to the Grahame-White factory in the First World War. Note the security on the gate and the wonderful polished brass sign to the left. (Barnet Local Studies)

Grahame-White Aviation built a great many different aircraft in sizeable quantities and were considered to be one of Britain's major aircraft constructors in the First World War. Production included twenty-four BE2 reconnaissance aircraft, 700 Airco DH5s, and 900 Avro 504s. The company employed a considerable workforce during the First World War, totalling 3,000 at its peak, and just like Airco nearby, these workers came from far and wide every day. In an attempt to secure their employment Grahame-White decided to have an estate built to house them. A site was chosen towards the end of Booth Road, with the buildings designed by Herbert Matthews. 'Aeroville', as it was named, began construction in 1917, and the original plan was to have a series of quadrangles with open space in the middle of each; however, by the time building stopped in 1919, only one had been finished, housing 300 workers. As time passed the homes were vacated and new residents moved in. Aeroville is praised as a good example of workers' housing and in 2010 it was listed by Historic England.

By 1918 Grahame-White owned 500 acres of land and 50 acres of buildings. Much like his peer George Holt Thomas at Airco, he had great plans for his aviation business after the war. He had assumed that the government would eventually hand back his aerodrome, together with a number of buildings they had taken control of, but sadly this was not to happen, and a bitter dispute carried on for years after the war. The government claimed contracts had not been met for a supply of DH.6 trainers; however the production had been held up because supplies of suitable timber had dried up. The aerodrome was only handed back to Grahame-White in 1920, but in this time he had lost revenue from flying activities. Eventually the government's Air Council took control of the aerodrome in 1926, whereupon it was renamed Royal Air Force Hendon.

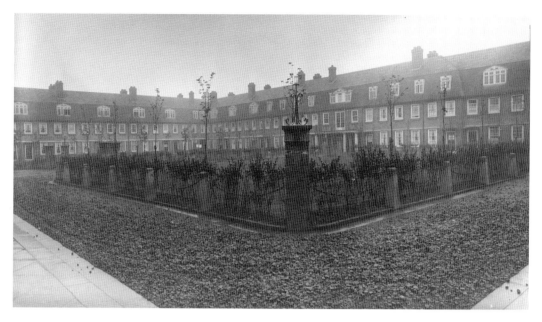

Above: The Grahame-White Company's Aeroville workers' housing in 1921. (Barnet Local Studies)

Below: Aeroville in 2021. (Author)

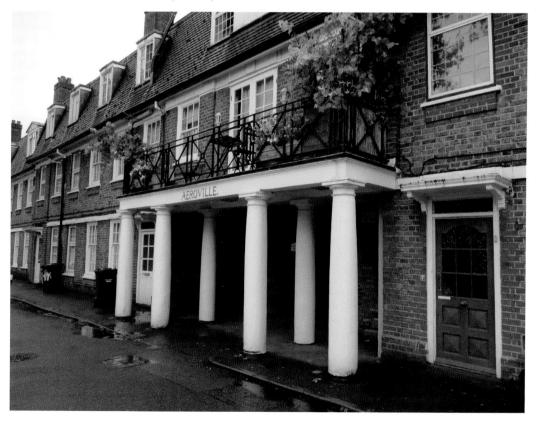

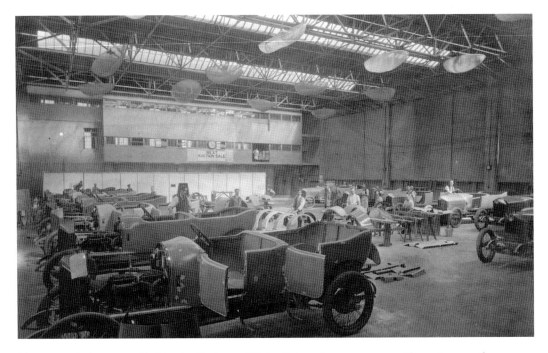

Motor cars being assembled in the Grahame-White factory hangar, *c.* 1920. The nets were there to collect insects attracted to the lighting. (Barnet Local Studies)

With orders for aircraft drying up after the end of the First World War, Grahame-White put his remaining employees to work, utilising the skills they had built on, in particular wood and metal working. The vast 1918 factory hangar was used for the building of car bodies, and for a short time the company even produced its own cyclecar. The company also produced furniture, and one of the contracts was for another part of Claude Grahame-White's post-war enterprises – the London Flying Club.

Despite losing control of his main aerodrome, Claude Grahame-White was not going to be defeated, and decided to use the area of land he had leased on the other side of Aerodrome Road for a small airfield and a sizeable club building. This was a well-appointed facility with a sixty-room hotel, restaurant, ballroom and bar, as well as thirty hard-surface tennis courts, two polo grounds and an eighteen-hole golf course. This was to be the place for well-heeled society to come out and spend time flying and generally having fun. By 1920 the London Flying Club had become a great success, with the hotel fully booked. However, it was just one of a number of flying clubs on the outskirts of London, other examples being the nearby Stag Lane, as well as probably the most famous at Brooklands, and despite the initial success, its popularity sadly declined. A further blow came in 1922 when the London Underground decided to extend the Hampstead and Highgate railway line (what is now called the Northern Line) from its Golders Green terminus out towards Edgware. A section of line from Hendon was to emerge from a tunnel, then out and around the perimeter of the London Flying Club, before reaching a new station at Colindale. By the time Colindale station opened in

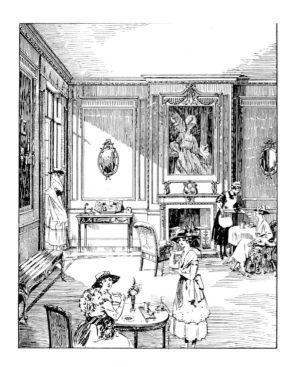

Ladies' Boudoir.

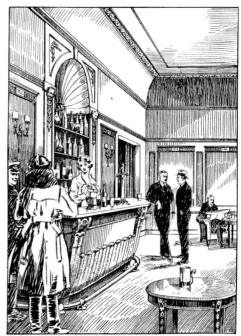

American Bar.

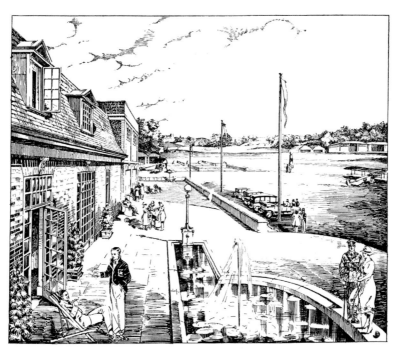

A view on the Club Terrace.

Illustrations of facilities at the London Flying Club, Hendon, from a Grahame-White publicity brochure. (Barnet Local Studies)

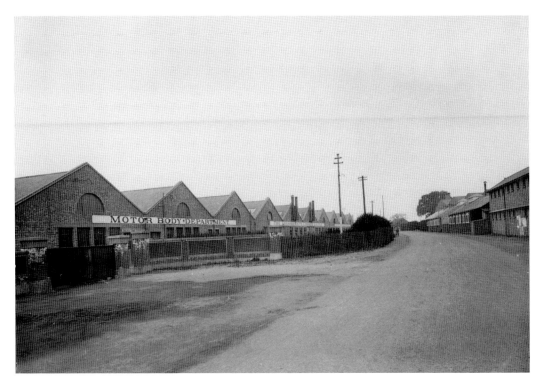

Aerodrome Road in 1920, showing the Grahame-White factories at a time when the company was involved in motor car production. These buildings were taken over by Standard Telephone & Cable a few years later. (Barnet Local Studies)

August 1924, the London Flying Club had effectively ceased flying activities and became the London Country Club. By 1925 Claude Grahame-White was carrying debt to the Inland Revenue from wartime government loans, and faced with this and a gradual realisation that the good times were coming to an end, he sought to sell and lease out his assets at Hendon. The Country Club was leased to Standard Telephone and Cables Limited to use as laboratories; the company also took over a number of the factory buildings. Other companies who moved into former Grahame-White buildings included the General Motors-owned electrical equipment manufacturer Delco, who were making early Frigidaire refrigeration equipment. The illuminated sign company Franco set up new workshops in 1922. Franco had taken their name from providing electric lighting decorations at the 1908 Franco-British Exhibition, and were responsible for much of the neon signage at Piccadilly Circus for many years. The firm of W. C. Gaunt used some of the former hangars on the airfield as a base for their Packard Cars concession. Aerodrome Road was also an early home for Aerofilms, a side business set up by Claude Grahame-White and his associate Francis Wills in 1919. Aerofilms undertook aerial photographic surveys for clients, and went on to be a highly successful concern, and a large part of its work is now to be found on the Britain from Above web resource. The Country Club's golf course was leased to Colindale Golf Club, and the former airfield was used for the grazing of sheep. Probably the saddest sales were those of Claude

Grahame-White's original pre-war aircraft, but saddest of all was the final settlement on Hendon aerodrome, with the government eventually paying Grahame-White around £500,000, according to some sources. However, despite first payments arriving in 1927, the money was not actually handed over to him in full until 1929. By this time Claude Grahame-White had finished in the aviation industry and moved abroad to concentrate on property businesses and his new interest with speed boats and yachts. He didn't lose ties with the aviation world though. He retained his Royal Aero Club membership, wrote a number of books and articles on the subject and would regularly return for aviation events. The grand old man of aviation, who had been at the start of it all, died in August 1959, at the age of eighty, in Nice, France – where his peer George Holt Thomas had passed away thirty years previously.

As time moved on the former Grahame-White buildings on the aerodrome side were taken over by the RAF. Meanwhile the former Country Club that had been used by Standard Telephone was eventually purchased by the Metropolitan Police, in 1934, to become their training college. In the early 1970s the old County Club buildings were pulled down when the police college facilities were modernised. Eventually most of the Grahame-White factory spaces were demolished, with the exception of a long building with a deep-gabled roof and a small tower on top, which served as a home to Aerofilms for a time. This structure, along with the 1917 mock-Tudor officers' mess on Grahame Park Way, are the only two Grahame-White-era buildings left on their original footprints. As a result of streamlining, the police facilities at Aerodrome Road were redeveloped between 2014

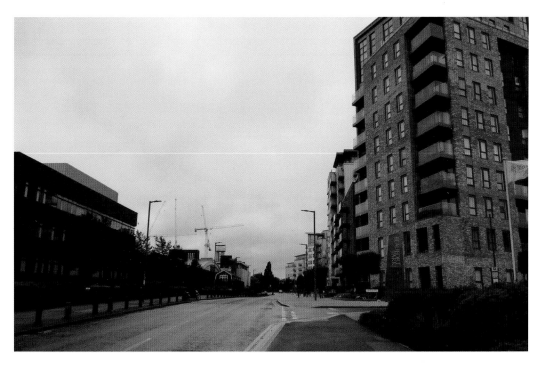

Aerodrome Road in 2021. To the right the Beaufort Park housing complex dwarfs the old Aerofilms building to the left of the road in the middle of the image. (Author)

and 2016, and a large chunk of land was sold to Redrow to create the Colindale Gardens residential development, most of it occupying what was originally the Country Club's golf course.

de Havilland

When Airco was sold to BSA in 1920, Geoffrey de Havilland decided he didn't want to work for the new owners, and with financial assistance from his old employer, George Holt Thomas, he set up his own aircraft company. The new manufacturer was to be called The de Havilland Aircraft Company Limited, and in the following forty years, until it's takeover by Hawker Siddeley in 1960, it was to be one of the most dynamic and forward-thinking British aircraft makers.

With the old Airco buildings on The Hyde now under the ownership of the BSA company, de Havilland needed a new home, and he didn't need to look too far. On the Edgware Road, at what is now Burnt Oak Broadway, there is a turning into Stag Lane. Just before the lane did a hard turn to the left, there was a recently vacated airfield with some wooden huts and canvas aircraft hangars. This had been the airfield for the London and Provincial Aviation Company, owned by William Warren and M. G. Smiles, who had initially started making Caudron aircraft under licence at Hendon Aerodrome in 1913; they also set up a successful flying school, occupying several hangars. By the time the First World War started the aerodrome at Hendon had become congested and in 1915 they moved up to Stag Lane, buying up land at Burnt Oak Farm for use as an airfield and flying school. When the war ended Warren and Smiles had used the old buildings to start a furniture-making business, and when this failed, they tried chocolate-making, again without great success. The two also hoped to carry on as a flying school; however they were ordered to leave Stag Lane in 1919, by the newly formed Department of Civil Aviation, over a dispute when a flying licence wasn't granted.

Arriving at Stag Lane on 5 October 1920, de Havilland and his team moved into the small collection of dilapidated wooden huts and hangars left by London and Provincial. The early winter months proved uncomfortable in a rather exposed part of semi-rural Middlesex. A 1957 copy of the *Hendon and Finchley Times* printed the reminiscences of a worker who had claimed that Geoffrey de Havilland would regularly tell the staff to go out and play football every so often, just to keep warm. The same report mentioned that a 'gypsy' woman who lived on the field provided hot meals to the company for the first year. It was a peculiar start for a company that would go on to great things in the next four decades.

In the first few years de Havilland was involved in the refurbishment and modification of ex-military aircraft. The company's output was almost entirely aimed at the emerging civilian market, with small, light aircraft for those who were taking up flying as a leisure pursuit. In 1925 the DH. Moth took its first flight, and from it developed a whole series of aircraft carrying the 'Moth' name, probably the most famous being the Tiger Moth. This legendary design took its first flight from Stag Lane in 1927, and the later trainer version went on to become the basic training aircraft for the Royal Air Force until the 1950s.

Stag Lane was sited in very much a semi-rural area, and in fact, with the exception of a row of late Victorian houses, the nearest building of any consequence was the Bald Faced Stag public house on the Edgware Road, just opposite the Stag Lane turning. This pub had

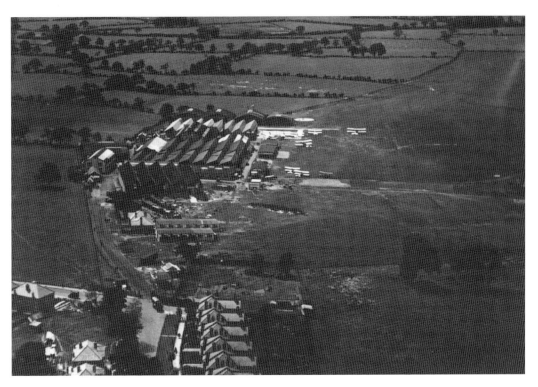

Stag Lane Aerodrome in 1927. This aerial image illustrates how the area was still semi- rural. (Barnet Local Studies)

once served the drivers of horse-drawn hay carts as they made their way to Central London, and it became a welcome watering hole for workers and fliers at Stag Lane Aerodrome.

In 1923 de Havilland set up their own School of Flying at Stag Lane, and it was used as a first point of basic training for those that would go on to be RAF Reserve officers. The airfield also attracted upwardly mobile men and women who wanted to fly their own aircraft as members of the London Aeroplane Club, established by de Havilland. Two notable examples were the couple Amy Johnson and Jim Mollison who used the aerodrome and flew de Havilland aircraft. Amy Johnson became a celebrity when she made her solo flight to Australia in 1930, and the aircraft she used was a de Havilland DH.60 Gipsy Moth, which she had named *Jason*. Her husband Jim Mollison left his mark in the area with a road that runs through Queensbury, named Mollison Way. In 1928 Stag Lane became home to the de Havilland Aeronautical Technical School, where training was provided to gain qualification to become a licensed Ground Engineer in the repair and maintenance of civil aircraft.

The first ten years at Stag Lane had seen Geoffrey de Havilland gradually build on his wartime achievements with Airco, to the point where his company had become a force to be reckoned with, producing evermore progressive designs and a dominant player in the civilian light aircraft market. By 1929 the workforce at Stag Lane numbered 1,500, and the company occupied a large number of new buildings on 15 acres of the site. In 1932 the company created the DH84 Dragon, a twin-engine, six-seat passenger light airliner, which became a mainstay of the pre-Second World War regional airlines. However, despite this

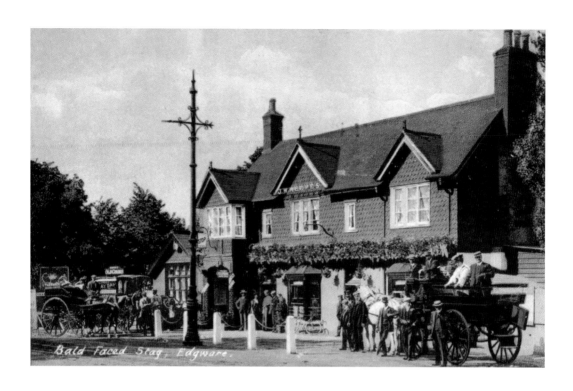

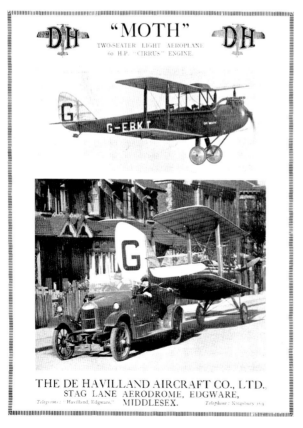

Above: The Bald Faced Stag public house in the 1910s. The pub was rebuilt around 1930. (Barnet Local Studies)

Left: 1925 press advertisement for de Havilland demonstrating the usability of their aircraft. The Morris car is seen towing a DH Moth along Colindale Avenue. The houses to the left are Nos 169–173, which still exist. (Aviation Ancestry)

success it was becoming clear that Stag Lane was not going to be suitable for the next stage of the company's growth. Just like Handley Page had been faced with suburban growth, so too had de Havilland. What had been open fields in 1920 was now encroached by a tide of housing that had been initiated by the extended London Underground railway to Edgware. This was to be accelerated by the extension of the Metropolitan Railway (the present Jubilee Line) from Wembley Park to Stanmore, which was begun in 1930 and opened in December 1932. Interestingly the new station on London Road at Stanmore was just a few yards away from The White House, the home of Geoffrey de Havilland since the First World War and until he passed way in 1965. (The house was replaced by a small estate of maisonettes in the late 1960s and renamed White House Close.) The line ran very close to Stag Lane, and it wasn't long before speculative builders started eyeing up the open land. Realising it was no longer feasible to keep the aerodrome, Geoffrey de Havilland had already started looking for a new home for his company and had found one at Hatfield in Hertfordshire, moving in gradually from 1930. A deal was done to sell the Stag Lane airfield to developers and by 1933 work was well underway on what became the new suburb of Queensbury, with the Metropolitan Railway opening a new station there in December 1934. The last aircraft to fly from Stag Lane was a DH Hornet Moth on 25 July 1934, piloted by Geoffrey de Havilland.

Though the Stag Lane factory buildings became surrounded by new suburban housing, the company decided to retain it for the building of aircraft engines and propellors, as well

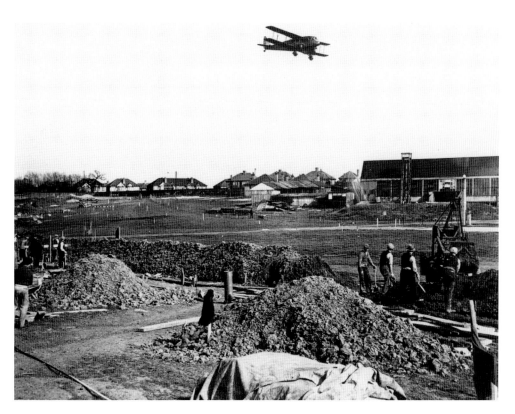

Final days of flying at Stag Lane. Builders look on as a DH Dragon comes in to land, c. 1933. Marker posts in the distance show the path of what will become De Havilland Way. (Brent Archives)

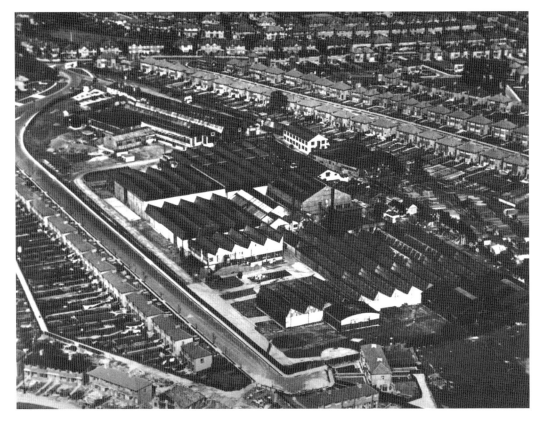

The de Havilland works in 1938. Suburban homes now surround the old aircraft hangars and factory buildings. (Barnet Local Studies)

as undertaking technical training. Geoffrey de Havilland's company continued to design and build increasingly advanced types of aircraft in the years that followed from the Mosquito fighter bomber of the Second World War to the world's first jet-powered airliner, the Comet. However, by 1960 the company was bought by Hawker Siddeley, who kept the name going for a further three years. Two years later, in May 1965, Geoffrey de Havilland passed away, at the age of eighty-two, at the Peace Memorial Hospital in Watford.

The Stag Lane factory continued under Hawker Siddeley's ownership, becoming part of the company's Bristol Siddeley aero engine division until the sale of this company to Rolls-Royce meant the facilities were surplus to requirement. In 1969 the site was sold to Brixton Estates who looked to rent out the vast factory spaces. The first tenant was BACS, the Banks Automated Clearing Service, set up in 1968 by the Inter-Bank Computer Bureau to speed up bulk payments between banks. The operation used the vast factory space to install their bulky computer equipment. In 1972 the second tenant arrived in the form of Post Office Telephones (the predecessor of BT), who needed a temporary home for their international call centre switching equipment whilst the permanent home, Mondial House, near Cannon Street, was being built. As a nod to the factory's past, the company named the two huge electronic exchange centres 'de Havilland' (Plessey TXK2) and 'Mollison' (Ericsson TXK5).

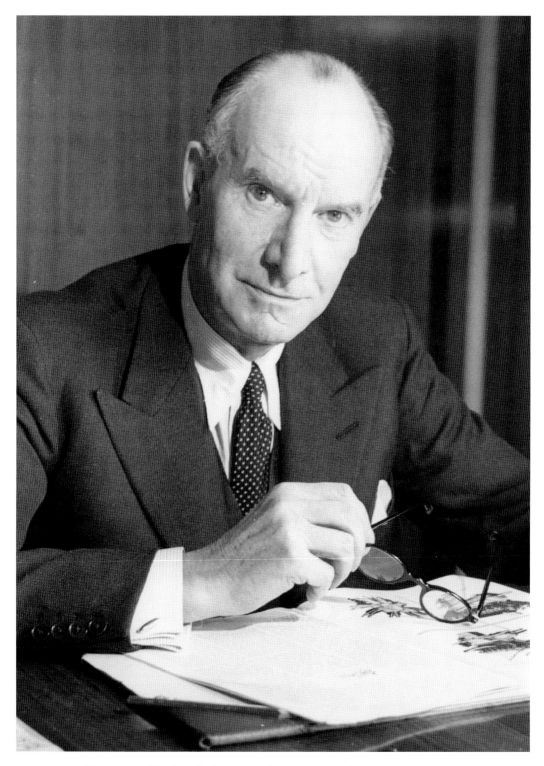

Sir Geoffrey de Havilland in the late 1940s. (Brent Archives)

British Telecom eventually moved out in 1988, and BACS in the late 1990s. The entire factory complex was then demolished to make way for a large estate of residential blocks. A plaque commemorating de Havilland and London & Provincial's years on the site was unveiled on 25 September 2000 on the side of one of the blocks, eighty years to the day of the incorporation of the de Havilland company. Cobham Close, Scott Road, Halford Close and De Havilland Road act as further reminders of the individuals associated with the aviation enterprise on the site.

Stag Lane was not the only de Havilland facility along the Edgware Road. The engine division took over the Car Mart showrooms and workshops near Staples Corner in the Second World War, as well as the Kemps biscuit factory nearby for aero engine work. The company also built a new factory complex on a former sports ground at Stonegrove, just past Edgware, in 1944. Here, under the management of long-term de Havilland man Frank Halford, development and production of the company's new 'Goblin' gas turbine jet engine took place. The Goblin engine was Britain's first successful jet engine and was fitted into de Havilland's Vampire jet fighter, which in turn became a great export for the company, selling to over thirty countries around the world. The factory lasted until the late 1940s and was then demolished to make way for the Stonegrove council housing development in the early 1950s. In turn this was redeveloped from 2014 onwards to become Barratt's 'Edgware Green' residential complex.

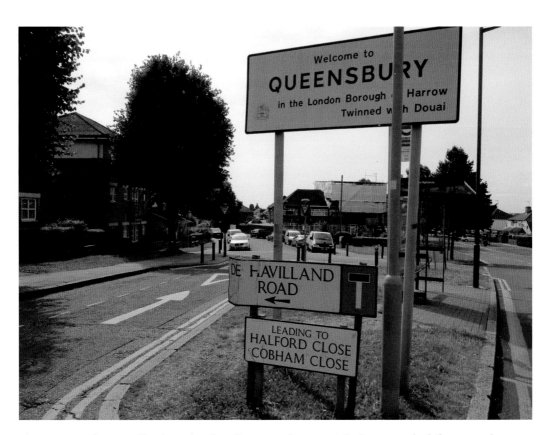

The junction of De Havilland Road and Mollison Road in 2021. The homes to the left occupy the site of the de Havilland works. (Author)

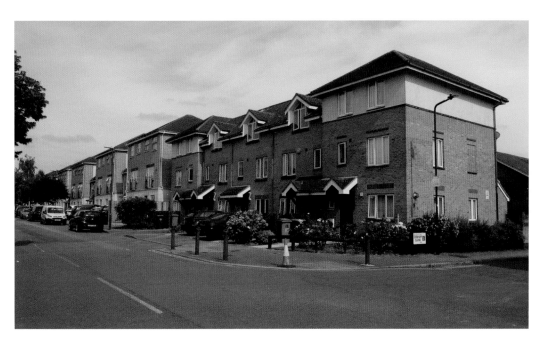

The view looking up De Havilland Road in 2021. The area in front of the houses would have been where the original aerodrome was. (Author)

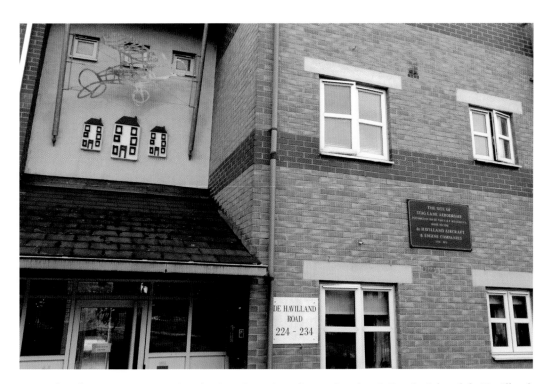

The plaque commemorating the Stag Lane Aerodrome, London & Provincial and de Havilland, on the side of housing erected in the late 1990s on the site of the former de Havilland works. (Author)

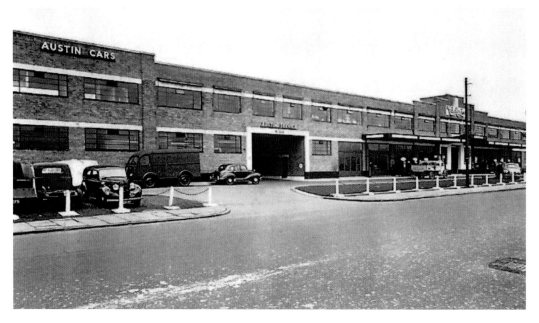

Late 1940s image of the Car Mart premises on the Edgware Road near Staples Corner, which was used by de Havilland in the Second World War. (David Whyley)

Hooper & Co.

Although not on the Edgware Road, Hooper & Co. were sited on a route that eventually led to it, in North Wembley, and are absolutely worthy of inclusion in this book.

Hooper & Company were a long-established coachbuilders, but like many adept companies they were contracted into war work. Being well versed in car body production, they were able to turn their skills very successfully into aircraft manufacture. Hooper built a new factory on East Lane, North Wembley, right next to the London Midland Railway line, in 1917. There they made Sopwith Camel fighters and parts for other aircraft. The site also had a small airfield next to the factory, some of which survives as a public park. Hooper made 375 Sopwith Camel F1s and thirty F21 Camels. There is a link between the Sopwith Camel and another great name on the Edgware Road. One of the two types of engine fitted to the aircraft was the Bentley BR.1, which was designed by W. O. Bentley, who went on to set up his own motor car factory, in 1920, on the junction of the Edgware Road and Oxgate Lane, in Cricklewood. The company was there until around 1930, having been bought by Rolls-Royce, and moved its production to Crewe.

The Hooper's site was later taken over by the General Electric Company (GEC) and was occupied by them right through to the 1990s. One of the main products made at North Wembley was GEC's 'Osram' light bulbs. After GEC left, part of the site was redeveloped into housing, but a considerable amount of the original buildings were repurposed into a business park.

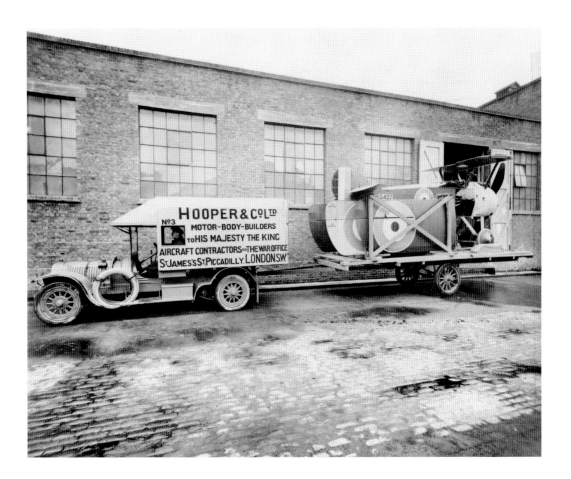

Above: Sopwith Camel B5407 on a trailer outside the Hooper & Co. works in North Wembley, 1917. This particular aircraft went on to serve with 66 Squadron RFC in Italy. (Brent Archives)

Right: Sopwith Camel fuselage sections under construction at Hooper & Co., North Wembley, 1917. (Brent Archives)

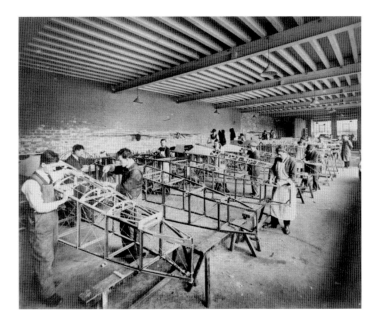

Associated Manufacturers & Suppliers

As well as the main aircraft makers, there were many other associated manufacturers along, and near, the Edgware Road who made a variety of vital elements that contributed towards the finished product.

L. A. Rumbold & Co.

L. A Rumbold & Co. made cabins, chairs and upholstery for aircraft, and were based in a factory on Kingsgate Place, which is just behind Kilburn High Road. In the Second World War they made parts for the de Havilland Mosquito. Any trace of their factory is long gone, with apartment blocks lining both sides of the narrow cobbled lane.

Whitlock Cars

In 1914 Goodman-Lawton intended manufacturing motor cars under the defunct name of Whitlock, at the Slade Works, which was at No. 135 Cricklewood Broadway. The Slade was originally an eighteenth-century farm that took its name from a brook that rose there. By the late nineteenth century, the farm had become a horse-centred business, with a riding school and private polo club. It was the livery stables and smithy that engineer and coachbuilder William Goodman-Lawton took over to start his Whitlock business. Before the company had a chance to do so, the First World War had started and the company concentrated on making motor ambulances for use on the battlefields of France. The company also made DH4 fuselages under contract for Airco. After the First World War Whitlock carried on making bodies for ambulances, ice-cream vans and mobile shops, and carried on doing so until 1991 when their lease expired. The factory was demolished and homes built on the site, accessed by the original entrance on the Broadway.

Smiths Aircraft Instruments

S. Smith and Sons Ltd were a well-established manufacturer of precision instruments and clocks established in Central London in 1851. They were quick to move into motor car instruments and gauges by the turn of the twentieth century. It was a natural progression to produce instrumentation for aircraft. The huge demand in production at the start of the First World War saw Smiths set up a new factory on Cricklewood Broadway in 1915, on land just before the railway bridge. It was a logical place to be, given the proximity of the three aircraft manufacturers, Handley Page, British Caudron and Nieuport and General (who had their factory just behind the Smiths site). The company continued at Cricklewood until the 1980s , after which the whole factory complex was cleared. The site is now occupied by a Matalan clothes store and a Wickes building supplies depot. Smiths Group Plc still exists as a successful international company in other locations in the UK and across the world.

Duple

Duple Motor Bodies were a bus and coach bodybuilder set up in 1919 at Hornsey, and moved to The Hyde, at West Hendon, in 1925. The site of the large factory was originally Cowleaze Farm. The company was very successful in the post-First World War years making motor coaches, trucks and vans for the new motorised road transport economy. In the Second World War, Duple, as part of the London Aircraft Production Group, made fuselage sections of Handley Page Halifax bombers. Duple closed its operations on The Hyde in 1970, having moved most of its operations to a factory in Blackpool in 1968. The West Hendon site was redeveloped into an industrial estate, and in the 1980s it became a Sainsbury's superstore. At the time of writing the site is being redeveloped for housing.

Titanine

The process of 'doping' the linen that covered the wings and fuselage of aircraft was vital to ensure the surfaces became taught and smooth, and on top of this were further layers of paint for decoration and camouflage. The company most closely associated with this process was Titanine Limited, and their factory was on the periphery of Hendon Aerodrome.

The origins of Titanine start with Holzapfel Compositions Company Limited, founded in Newcastle upon Tyne in 1881. The company had started out making coatings for the nearby shipbuilding industry. By 1915 Holzapfel had developed coatings for the aircraft industry and had set up a separate company to do this called The British Aeroplane Varnish Company Limited. It seemed only natural to locate this new concern closer to one of the biggest hubs of aircraft manufacture, and so they built a small set of buildings at the end of what is now Sheaveshill Avenue. In 1918 the company changed its name to 'Titanine', making a clear reference to its product's ability to strengthen. During the course of the First

World War, the company had produced over one million gallons of doping varnish – quite how many aircraft that covered is not easy to calculate, but it would have probably been thousands.

In 1921 Titanine purchased its competitor British Emaillite, who had a factories in Willesden Junction, Stonebridge and Shepherds Bush, and the new company was renamed Titanine-Emaillite Ltd. After the Second World War, doping varnish was not required by an industry that used metal to cover aircraft structures; however paints and finishes were still needed. In the 1950s Titanine developed the white anti-flash coatings used on the V-bomber force, in particular for the Handley Page Victor whose major parts were manufactured at Cricklewood.

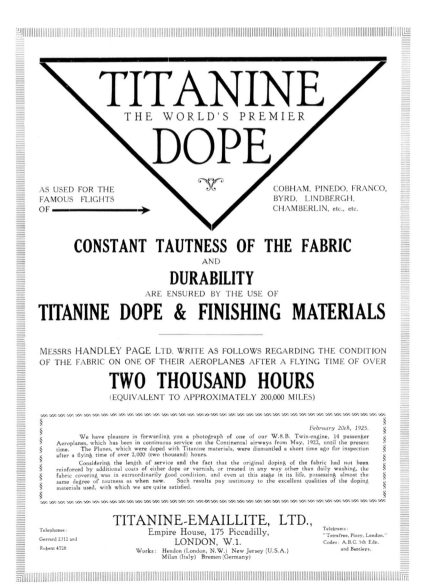

Titanine press ad from the 1920s. (Barnet Local Studies)

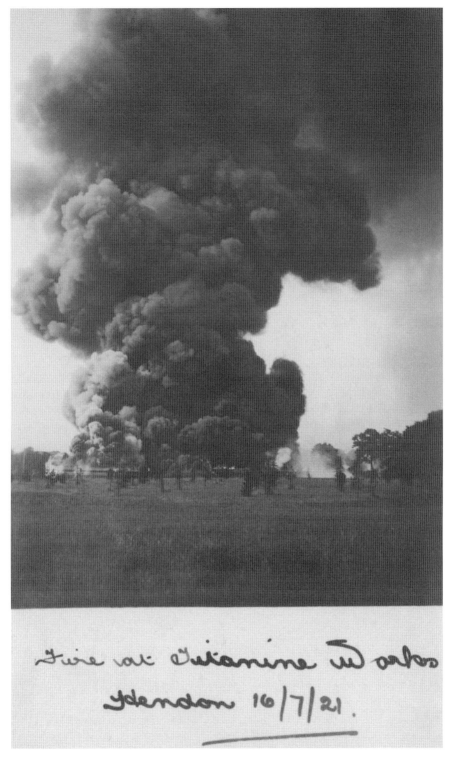

Fire at Titanine Works Hendon 16/7/21.

Huge clouds of smoke rising from the Titanine works, Hendon, 16 July 1921. (Barnet Local Studies)

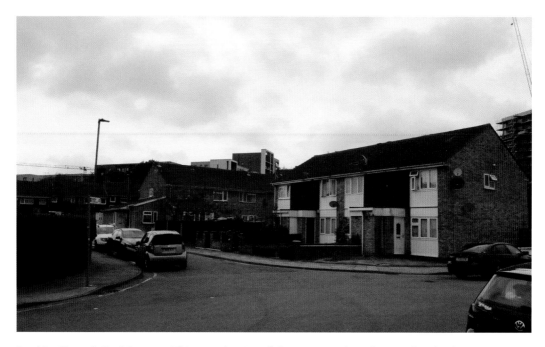

Rankin Close, Colindale, 2021. This was the site of the Titanine dope factory. (Author)

A factory producing such a potentially combustible and explosive product was bound to have accidents. In the hot summer of 1921, a huge fire took place and the events were caught on camera by the Topical Budget newsreel company. Their captions described the events as a 'Volcanic spectacle', with 'Fires like Vesuvius'. This remarkable short film is available to view for free on the British Film Institute's BFI Player. In September 1948 a fire raged for two hours as flames rose up to 200 feet, with exploding barrels of butyl alcohol hurled into the air, and as a result hundreds of local residents were forced to vacate their homes. The company's own fire brigade and the local brigade eventually brought the fire under control. Such incidents happening in a built-up area could not be allowed to continue, and by the mid-1960s Titanine had closed the factory and moved its activities back to the parent company's site in Tyne and Wear. The Colindale factory site is now covered by a small estate of late 1960s homes called Rankin Close.

Overview

Over the course of this book, I have attempted to condense a great deal of history into a digestible read. My hope was to show how the arrival of aviation in the first decade of the twentieth century played a major part in changing what was to become north-west London.

Before the aeronautical world made its impact, much of the surrounding areas along the Edgware Road, past Cricklewood, were semi-rural, with most employment connected to agriculture, in particular haymaking and dairy farming, as well as trades like blacksmithing and woodworking. The pioneers who arrived with their primitive aeroplanes were merely looking for a conveniently located space to develop their ambitions. To local people these individuals were considered as either daring adventurers or eccentric oddballs. It was only with the establishment of the London Aerodrome that there was a gradual acceptance of this exciting new form of conveyance. Regular public air displays brought large numbers of curious visitors to this part Middlesex, with most of them travelling along the Edgware Road to get there. Within six years the area had established itself as a place of wonder and fun, and Hendon forged its long association with flying.

The arrival of the First World War meant that Hendon became the focus for military aviation. Gone was the fun and frivolity, replaced by the need to train pilots for conflict, and rapid industrialisation of aircraft manufacture. Vast new factories were built over the semi-rural landscape, bringing with it, eventually, more buildings. The creation of jobs for many thousands of workers, in particular women, in the aircraft factories opened new possibilities. New skills were learnt and new methods of working, especially that of an 'assembly line', where the individual processes of mass production were broken down into a series of tasks, with individuals working on their own area, contributing to the finished item. These were concepts that were in their infancy in the early twentieth century; it was a time before the occurrence of mass-produced products such as motor cars and household goods, and it was the First World War that fine-tuned these ideas. The need for constantly improved designs and the high losses of aircraft meant better machines in higher numbers were demanded all the time. It took a war to gear up the concept of efficient, rapid production, and it was these new ideas that would carry on into the interwar period, when the new consumer age effectively began.

Although the aircraft industry carried on in the area with Handley Page and de Havilland, it was considerably smaller in the immediate years after the First World War. This situation and the eventual closing down of Airco, Grahame-White, Nieuport and Caudron meant that there was a great deal of available manufacturing space. It would not be long before new industries took these redundant spaces over, and that repurposing led to the Edgware Road, along its length, contributing to London's manufacturing as a whole. The rapid post-war industrialisation was matched by housebuilding and population growth. By the time the Second World War had started, the route taken in 1901 would look totally different, and so much of that was down to aviation. In this second conflict Handley Page at Cricklewood was the sole survivor of the original manufacturers making warplanes, but there were many sub-contracted factories, like Duple at West Hendon, turning out parts that would contribute to the aircraft industry. In the post-war years industry and local workers continued their contributions to aviation, but by the time Hendon Aerodrome closed in the late 1950s, the glory years were long gone. The eventual decline of manufacturing along the Edgware Road saw factories close, and with them jobs. The closure of Handley Page in 1965 marked an end to aviation manufacturing in the area, but it also saw the creation of the Greater London Council, and former parts of Middlesex became London boroughs.

The Edgware Road is now bereft of industry, most of the factory buildings have gone, replaced by the metal sheds of retail, warehousing and distribution of things made outside of Britain, and more recently by high-density apartment complexes. The last vestiges of the area's aviation past are preserved at the wonderful Royal Air Force Museum and a few murals, plaques and road names. Within the space of 100 years the wonders of flying had come and gone. Now the only aeroplanes that pass over the Edgware Road are airliners flying in and out of London's five airports, the passengers inside oblivious to the contribution the area below them made towards aviation history.

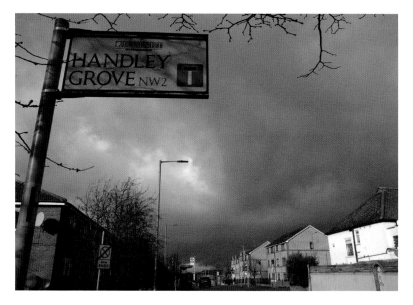

Handley Grove sign on Claremont Road, Cricklewood, 2022. The housing in the distance is on the site of the Handley Page works. (Author)

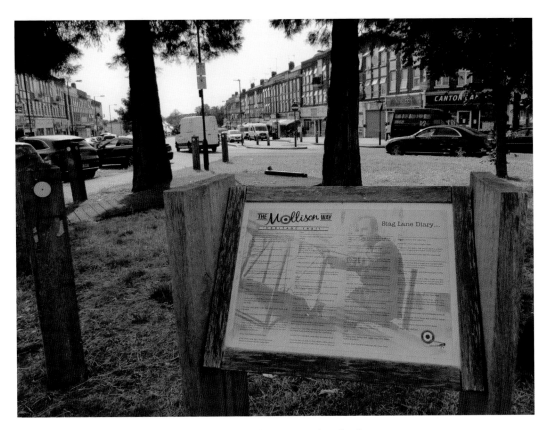

Heritage board on Mollison Way, Queensbury, 2021. (Author)

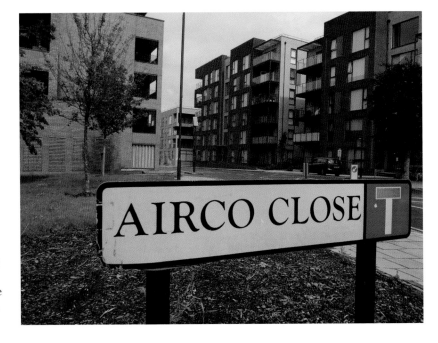

Airco Close, off Grove Park, Colindale, 2021. The apartments on the other side of the road are The Silverworks. (Author)

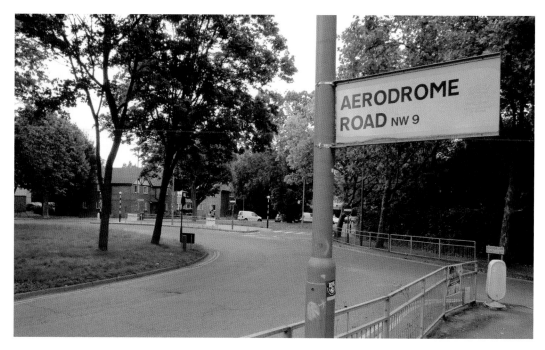

The roundabout at the end of Colindale Avenue, 2021. The crossings in the distance are approximately where the entrance gates to RAF Hendon once were. (Author)

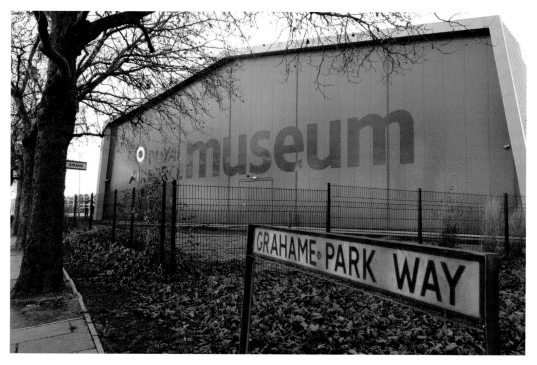

The exterior of the Royal Air Force Museum, from Grahame Park Way, 2021. The building you can see was opened in 1978 as the Battle of Britain Hall. (Author)

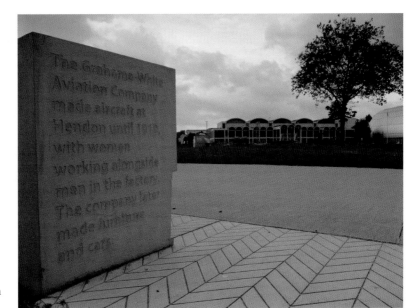

A concrete memorial seat at the RAF Museum, Hendon. The building in the distance is the main museum, which opened in 1972. (Author)

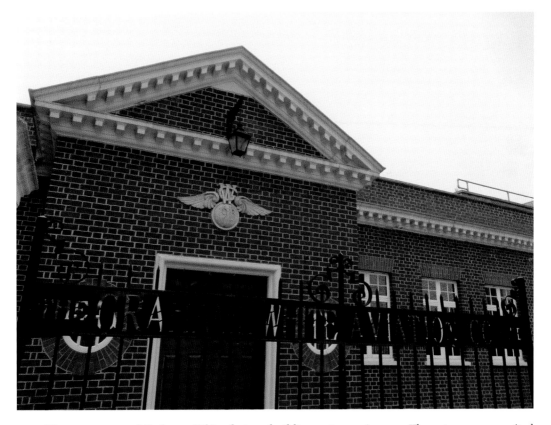

The reconstructed Grahame-White factory building entrance in 2021. The gates were reunited with the building having spent many years as part of perimeter fencing for the RAF Museum. (Author)

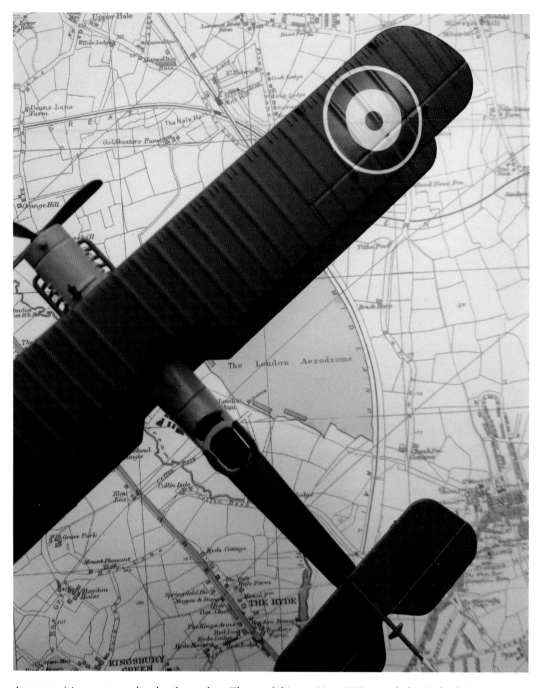

A composition put together by the author. The model is an Airco DH 4 made by Oxford Diecast 'flying' over Bacon's 1912 map of London. (Author)

Bibliography

Airco Rag magazine, 1919

Barnes, C. H., *Handley Page Aircraft since 1907* (Putnam, 1976)

Clifford, John, *de Havilland and Hatfield 1910–1935* (Fonthill, 2015)

de Havilland Aeronautical Technical School at Stag Lane and Kingsbury – www.dhaetsa.org.uk

Davies, Mick, *Airco: The Aircraft Manufacturing Company* (Crowood Press, 2001)

Flight Magazine, 23 October 1914

Graces Guide (online)

Hendon Borough Council, *A History of Hendon* (1964)

Langham, Rob, *Bloody Paralyser: The Giant Handley Page Bombers of the First World War* (Fonthill, 2016)

Moher, James, *Scourge of the Fokkers* (JGM Books, 2017)

Oliver, David, *Hendon Aerodrome: A History* (Airlife, 1994)

Renwick, Andrew, *RAF Hendon: The Birthplace of Aerial Power* (Flight Recorder Publications, 2012)

Scott, David & Ian Simmons, *George Holt Thomas: The Man Who Created Airco* (self-published, 2018)

Shute, Nevil, *Slide Rule* (Pan Books, 1968)

Smith, Ron, *British Built Aircraft, Greater London* (Tempus, 2002)

Smith, Sally, *Magnificent Women and Flying Machines* (History Press, 2021)

Victoria County History, London, *A History of the County of Middlesex: Vol 5*

Acknowledgements

With thanks to Philip Jarrett, Hugh Petrie at Barnet Archives, Alan Dowsett of the Handley Page Association, Dave Scott, Stuart McKay, John Alsop, Royal Air Force Museum, Kwik Fit (Colindale), Barclays Group Archive, Graces Guide, Dick Weindling and Marianne Colloms, Rabbi Silverman and the Beis Yaakov School, Dave Robinson at Aviation Ancestry, and Lukas Novotny.